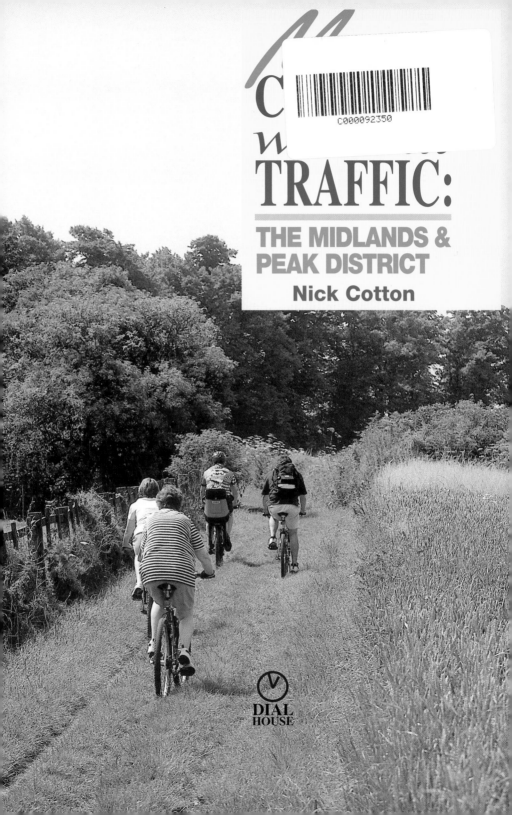

CYCLING WITHOUT TRAFFIC:

THE MIDLANDS & PEAK DISTRICT

Nick Cotton

DIAL
HOUSE

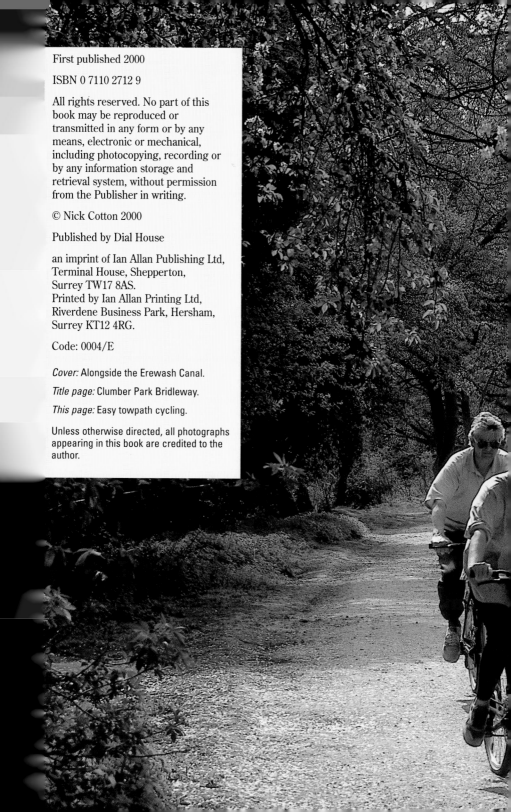

First published 2000

ISBN 0 7110 2712 9

Published by Dial House

an imprint of Ian Allan Publishing Ltd,
Terminal House, Shepperton,
Surrey TW17 8AS.
Printed by Ian Allan Printing Ltd,
Riverdene Business Park, Hersham,
Surrey KT12 4RG.

Code: 0004/E

Cover: Alongside the Erewash Canal.

Title page: Clumber Park Bridleway.

This page: Easy towpath cycling.

CONTENTS ᚛

More and more people are realising that cycling is good for both health and well-being. The government has started showing a real interest in promoting cycling as a way of solving transport problems, and the National Cycle Network will soon have a major effect by helping to change lifestyles and people's mode of transport. However, vehicle numbers are still increasing which means that even minor lanes can become busy with traffic — you can very rarely be guaranteed to find the safety, peace and quiet that are the essential ingredients of a family bike ride on the road network.

This book describes 30 routes, most of them easy and waymarked, where you can cycle away from traffic, and gives further information about where to ride and how to obtain cycling leaflets produced by local authorities and other organisations.

This Spread: Get away from it all on a bike.

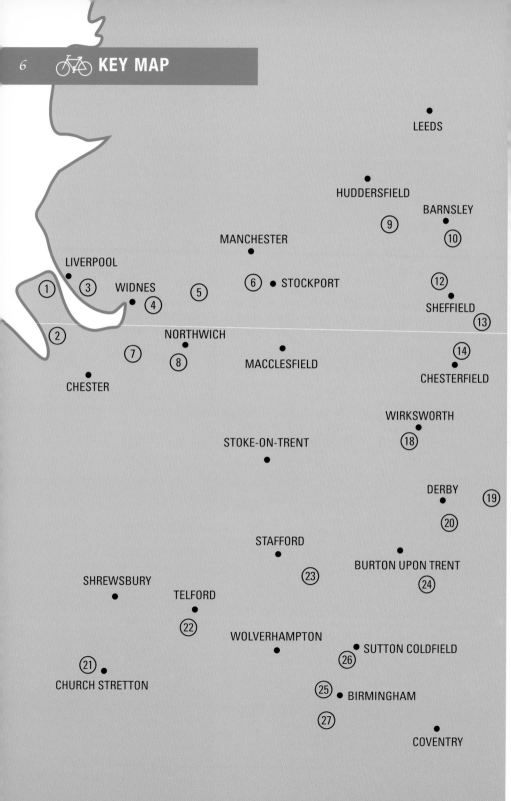

LEEDS

HUDDERSFIELD

BARNSLEY

⑨

⑩

MANCHESTER

⑫

LIVERPOOL

① ③ WIDNES ⑤ ⑥ ● STOCKPORT

SHEFFIELD

④

⑬

② NORTHWICH

⑭

⑦ ⑧

MACCLESFIELD

CHESTERFIELD

CHESTER

WIRKSWORTH

STOKE-ON-TRENT

⑱

DERBY

⑲

⑳

STAFFORD

BURTON UPON TRENT

SHREWSBURY ⑳ ㉓ ㉔

TELFORD

㉒

WOLVERHAMPTON

SUTTON COLDFIELD

㉑ ㉖

CHURCH STRETTON

㉕ ● BIRMINGHAM

㉗

COVENTRY

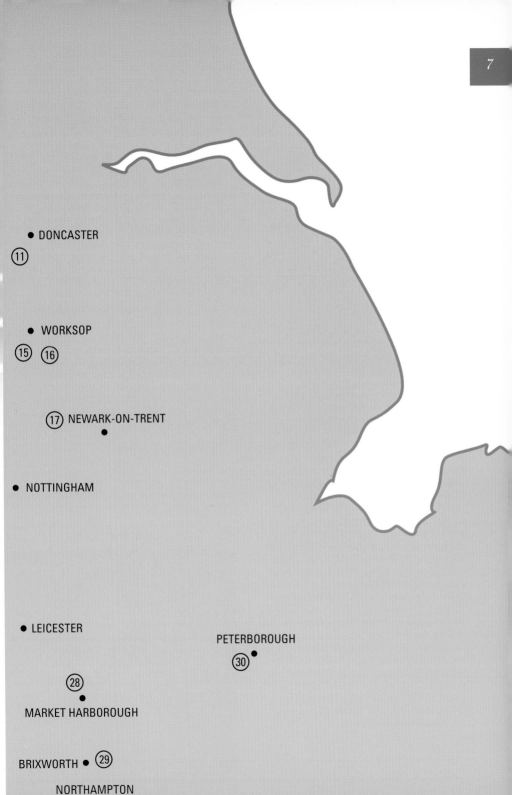

The first volume of *Cycling Without Traffic: The Midlands & Peak District* proved to be so popular that it seemed a good idea to produce a second volume with a further 30 traffic-free rides covering this area of the country. In the time that has elapsed between researching the first and second volumes many local authorities have produced high-quality traffic-free routes, often in conjunction with Sustrans (it stands for Sustainable Transport), an engineering charity based in Bristol which was awarded £43 million by the National Lottery in 1995 to create the National Cycle Network. See below for more details.

The trails can be divided into five categories:

1. DISMANTLED RAILWAYS

The vast majority of Britain's railway system was built in the 50 years from 1830 to 1880. After the invention of the car and the development of the road network from the turn of the 20th century onwards, the railways went into decline and in the 1960s many of the lines were closed and the tracks lifted. This was the famous 'Beeching Axe'. It is a great tragedy that Dr Beeching was not a keen leisure cyclist! Had he set in motion the development of leisure cycle trails along the course of the railways he was so busy closing then we could boast one of the finest recreational cycling networks in the world.

As it is, many of the railways were sold off in small sections to adjacent landowners and the continuity of long sections of dismantled track was lost. Almost 40 years on, some local authorities (notably the Peak District) have risen to the challenge and created some fine trails along the course of the dismantled railways. Within this book the Dove Valley Trail, the Derby to Worthington Railway Path and the Silkin Way in Telford are all good examples. The first *Cycling Without Traffic: The Midlands & Peak District* covered other popular railway paths in the region such as the High Peak and Tissington Trails in the Peaks, the Brampton Valley Way near Northampton and the Stratford Greenway south of Stratford-upon-Avon.

To find out what your own authority intends to do in the future about cycle trails in your area, contact the planning department of your county council (see Useful Addresses page 109-10). Alternatively, if you wish to get involved on a national level, contact Sustrans, 35 King Street, Bristol BS1 4DZ (Tel: 0117 929 0888), the organisation building the 10,000-mile National Cycle Network which will be completed in the year 2005.

Dismantled railways make good cycle trails for two reasons. Firstly, the gradients tend to be very gentle, and secondly, the broad stone base is ideal for the top dressing which creates a smooth firm surface for bicycles. Twelve of the 30 rides in this book use dismantled railways for all or part of the ride.

2. COUNTRY PARKS

Certain country parks are either big enough to have trails running through them or else the network of the roads within the park has so little traffic (which tends to be slow-moving and highly aware of cyclists) that they have also been included within this guide. The parks tend to have all sorts of other attractions, too. At Tatton Park and Clumber Park there is a charge for both the car park and the attractions.

3. FORESTRY COMMISSION LAND

There are seven waymarked trails on Forestry Commission land in the area covered by this book:

Below: Cycling keeps you fit and healthy.

There are hundreds of miles of forest tracks to explore.

1. Wharncliffe Wood, near Sheffield (Route 12, page 48).
2. Clipstone Forest in the Sherwood Forest Country Park, north of Nottingham (covered in the first *Cycling Without Traffic: The Midlands & Peak District*).
3. Delamere Forest, east of Chester (Route 7, page 34).
4. Cannock Chase, north of Birmingham (Route 23, page 78).
5. Colstey Woods/Bury Ditches, Shropshire (25 miles south of Shrewsbury, Grid Reference 334838).
6. Eastridge Woods/Habberley/Poles Coppice car park (10 miles southwest of Shrewsbury, Grid Reference 386043).
7. Hopton Woods near Craven Arms, Shropshire (10 miles west of Ludlow, Grid Reference 350779).

As a general rule, it is permissible to cycle on the hard forestry tracks in other woodland owned by the Forestry Commission, but there are some exceptions. The chapter on the Forestry Commission (see page 106-7) gives details of the locations of their sites, and addresses and phone numbers of regional offices so that you can find out the exact regulations (which may change at any time due to logging operations).

4. CANAL TOWPATHS

The British Waterways Board has undertaken a national survey of its 2,000 miles of towpath to see what percentage is suitable for cycling. Unfortunately, the initial results are not very encouraging — only about 10% meet the specified requirements. In certain cases regional waterways boards have co-ordinated with local authorities and the Countryside Commission to improve the towpaths for all users. It is to be hoped that this collaboration continues and extends throughout the country.

Cycling along canal towpaths can provide plenty of interest — wildlife, barges and locks — and the gradient tends to be flat. However, even the best-quality towpaths are not places to cycle fast as they are often busy with anglers and walkers and it is rare that cycling two-abreast is feasible.

The chapter on canals (see page 104-6) gives you a map of the canal network in the Midlands and details of the Waterways Boards to contact for further information about the towpaths nearest to you.

5. RESERVOIRS

Large reservoirs can sometimes provide excellent cycling opportunities: the rides are circular, the setting is often very beautiful and there is the added attraction of waterfowl to see. Two rides around reservoirs are described in full: one covers Carsington Reservoir, near Ashbourne, and the other Pitsford Water, north of Northampton. Both are relatively new reservoirs, built in the last 10 years and both have cycle hire outlets.

OTHER CYCLING ROUTES

If you wish to venture beyond the relatively protected world of cycle trails, there are two choices: either write away for leaflets produced by local authorities describing rides on quiet lanes through the countryside (details are given on page 109-10), or devise your own route.

Should you choose the second course, study the relevant Ordnance Survey Landranger map; the yellow roads represent the smaller, quieter lanes. When cycling off-road, you must stay on legal rights of way. It is illegal to cycle on footpaths, but you are allowed to use bridleways, byways open to all traffic (BOATS) and roads used as public paths (RUPPS). These are all marked on Ordnance Survey maps. Devising routes 'blind' can sometimes be a bit of a hit-or-miss affair, however. Some tracks may turn out to be very muddy and overgrown, and other hazards include blocked paths, locked gates and inadequate or non-existent waymarking. If you feel strongly about the condition of a right of way, contact the Rights of Way Department of your local authority and report the problems you have found.

Left: No cars, no traffic, no problem!

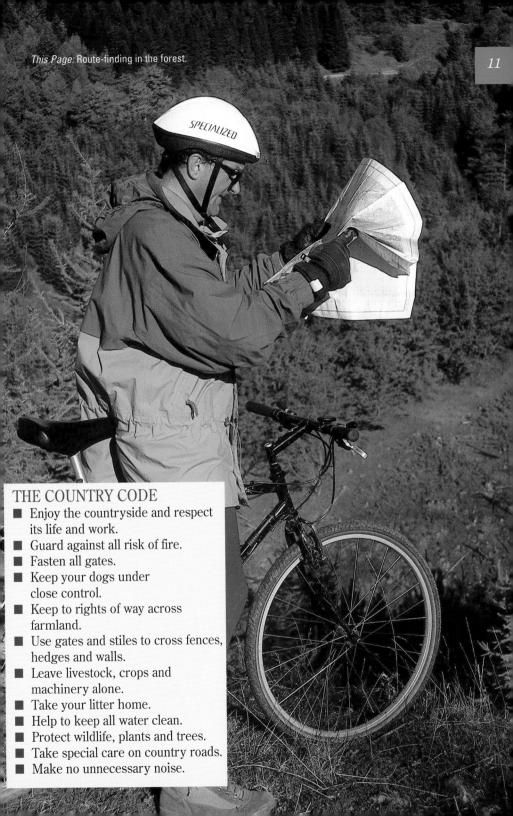

THE COUNTRY CODE

- Enjoy the countryside and respect its life and work.
- Guard against all risk of fire.
- Fasten all gates.
- Keep your dogs under close control.
- Keep to rights of way across farmland.
- Use gates and stiles to cross fences, hedges and walls.
- Leave livestock, crops and machinery alone.
- Take your litter home.
- Help to keep all water clean.
- Protect wildlife, plants and trees.
- Take special care on country roads.
- Make no unnecessary noise.

Bicycles should be thoroughly overhauled on a regular basis but there are certain things worth checking before each ride, and knowledge of how to mend a puncture is essential.

The four most important things to check are:

1. Do both the front and rear brakes work effectively?
2. Are the tyres inflated hard?
3. Is the chain oiled?
4. Is the saddle the right height?
   (Low enough when sitting in the saddle to be able to touch the ground with your toes; high enough to have your leg almost straight when you are pedalling.)

Other clickings, grindings, gratings, crunchings, rattling, squeakings, wobblings and rubbings either mean that your bike needs oiling and parts need adjusting, or a trip to your local bike mechanic is long overdue. Try to give a bike shop as much warning as possible; do not expect to turn up and have your bike fixed on the spot.

Right: Regular checks keep the bike working smoothly. *Simon Joslin*

Essential kit for a bike ride.

MENDING A PUNCTURE

You will need:
- a spanner to undo the nuts holding the wheel to the frame.
- tyre levers to ease the tyre off the rim.
- glue and patches.
- a pump.

These items should always be carried, even on short rides, as walking with a bike with a flat tyre is not much fun.

1. Remove the wheel which has the puncture, using a spanner to undo the nuts on the hub if it is not fitted with quick-release levers (you will probably have to unhitch the brake cable in order to remove the wheel).

2. Remove the tyre from the rim, using tyre levers if the fit is tight. Insert two levers under the rim a few inches apart and push on them together to free the tyre from the rim, taking care not to pinch the inner tube. Work the levers around the rim until the tyre is completely free.

3. Remove the dust cap and any locking ring from the valve. Push the valve inside the tyre then gently pull the inner tube out.

4. Partially inflate the tyre and pass it close to your ear until you hear a hiss (or close to your cheek or lips to feel the escaping air). Locate the puncture and mark it with a cross, using the crayon you should have in the puncture repair kit. (It is not often that you need to use a bucket of water to locate a puncture: you can almost always hear it or feel it.)

5. Deflate the tyre, by pushing in the valve. Hold the tyre so that the section with the puncture is tight over your knuckles. If you have sandpaper in the repair kit, lightly roughen the area around the puncture.

6. Spread glue thinly over the puncture, covering an area slightly larger than the patch you are going to use. **Leave to dry for at least five minutes.** This is the stage at which many people go wrong: they try to fix the patch too soon. The glue is not an adhesive, it is actually melting the rubber.

7. While waiting for the glue to do its stuff, check the inside of the tyre for any obvious thorn or piece of glass which may have caused the puncture. Run your finger slowly and sensitively around the inside of the tyre to see if you can find the cause of the puncture.

8. After waiting at least five minutes for the glue, select a patch, remove the foil and push the patch firmly into the middle of the gluey area. Peel off the backing paper. If you have a lump of chalk in the repair kit, dust the area with some grated chalk.

9. Replace the tube inside the tyre, starting by pushing the valve through the hole in the rim. Ensure that the tube is completely inside the tyre, then using only your hands (ie NOT the tyre levers) gently ease the tyre back inside the rim. The last section will be the hardest; use the heel of the palms of your hands and your thumbs to roll the last part back inside the rim.

10. Re-inflate the tyre, replace the locking ring and the dust cap. Replace the wheel into the frame of the bike and do the nuts up tightly, ensuring that it is set centrally (check by spinning the wheel and seeing if it rubs against the frame). Re-attach the brakes if you have detached the cable.

Top: Punctures can happen to anybody!

BICYCLE HIRE

Some of the more popular cycling areas now have bike-hire centres, notably at the larger reservoirs and some of the designated Forestry Commission trails. They offer a good opportunity to test different bikes, to give a non-cyclist a chance of trying out cycling, or can save the hassle of loading up and carrying your own bikes to the start of a trail. Wherever cycle-hire centres exist, they are mentioned in the route descriptions in the Essential Information section. It is a good idea to ring beforehand and book a bike, particularly on summer weekends and during the school holidays.

Top: Cycle Hire at Pitsford Water, Northampton.

Above: Cycle trailer at Clumber Park.

Right: Many Forest Visitor Centres hire out bikes.

Comfort, freedom of movement and protection against the unexpected shower should be the three guiding factors in deciding what to wear when you go cycling. Specialist cycling clothing is by no means essential to enjoy cycling, particularly on the short and easy rides contained in this book.

HELMET AND HEADGEAR

The issue of wearing helmets often provokes controversy. Let us hope that it forever remains a matter of personal choice. A helmet does not prevent accidents from happening. Nevertheless, most serious injuries to cyclists are head injuries and helmets can reduce impact.

The case for children wearing helmets is much stronger: they are far more likely to cause damage to themselves by losing control and falling over than an adult. It may be difficult at first to avoid the strap 'pinching' when putting a helmet on a child's head. Bribery of some form or other, once the helmet is securely in place, often helps to persuade the child to see the helmet as a good thing.

In cold weather, a woolly hat or a balaclava is the most effective way of keeping warm. Twenty per cent of body heat is lost through the head.

THE UPPER BODY

It is better to have several thin layers of clothing rather than one thick sweater or coat so that you can make fine adjustments to achieve the most comfortable temperature. Zips or buttons on sleeves and the front of garments also allow you to adjust the temperature.

Try putting your arms right out in front of you — is the clothing tight over your back? If so, you should wear something a bit looser.

If you are intending to cycle regularly when it is cold, it is worth investing in good-quality thermal underwear and synthetic fleece jackets. These help perspiration to dissipate, do not hold water and dry quickly.

A small woollen scarf and gloves (together with the woolly hat mentioned above) take up very little space and enable you to cope with quite a drop in temperature.

WATERPROOFS

You are far more at risk from exposure on a wet and windy day than a cold, dry day. The biggest danger lies in getting thoroughly soaked when a strong wind is blowing. Unless you are absolutely certain that it will not rain, it is always worth packing something waterproof. A light, showerproof cagoule takes up little space. If you are buying a waterproof top specifically for cycling, buy a very bright coloured jacket with reflective strips so that you are visible when light is poor.

Top: Wear clothing that lets you move freely.

LEGS

As with the upper body, what you should be looking for is something comfortable which does not restrict your movement. Tight, non-stretch trousers would be the worst thing to wear — uncomfortable at the knees and the hips and full of thick seams that dig in! Baggy track suit bottoms tend to get caught in the chain and can hold a lot of water if it rains. The best things to wear are leggings or tracksters that are fairly tight at the ankle. However, if you feel reluctant about looking like a ballet dancer, then a long pair of socks worn over the bottom of your trousers keeps them from getting oily or caught in the chain.

CYCLING SHORTS

If you are going to do a lot of cycling then cycling shorts should be the first piece of specialist clothing you buy. They give a lot of padding while allowing your legs to move freely.

FOOTWEAR

Almost any shoe with a reasonably flat sole is appropriate, although you should bear in mind that few of the trails are sealed with tarmac so there may well be puddles or even mud in some cases after rain.

A pair of trainers or old tennis shoes are a good bet.

NB Take care to ensure that shoe laces are tied and are not dangling where they could get caught in the chain. The same goes for straps on backpacks and straps on panniers, or particularly long scarves!

WHAT TO TAKE

- Hat, scarf, gloves.
- Waterproof.
- Drink (water or squash is better than fizzy drinks).
- Snacks (fruit, dried fruit, nuts, malt loaf, oatbars).
- Tool kit (pump, puncture repair kit, small adjustable spanner, reversible screwdriver, set of Allen keys, tyre levers, chain link extractor).
- Guide book and map (map holder).
- Money.
- Camera.
- Lock.
- Lights and reflective belt (if there is the remotest possibility of being out after dusk).

You can either carry the above in a day-pack on your back or in panniers that fit on to a rack at the rear of the bike. Panniers are the best bet as they do not restrict your movement and do not make your back sweaty.

Top: Several thin layers of clothing are best.

Left: Specialist clothing isn't necessary on these easy rides.

In theory there are three ways of getting to the start of a ride: cycling there from home; catching a train and cycling to your start point; or carrying the bikes on a car. If you drive, there are three ways of transporting the bikes.

INSIDE THE CAR

With quick-release skewers now fitted on many new bikes (on the saddle and wheels), it is usually easy to take bikes apart quickly and to fit them into the back of most hatchback cars. If you are carrying more than one bike inside the car you should put an old blanket between each bike to protect paintwork and delicate gear mechanisms from damage.

If you would like to carry your bike(s) inside your car and the idea of quick-release skewers appeals to you, these can normally be fitted by your local bike shop.

Bear in mind that the bikes may be wet and/or muddy when you get back to the car so carry sheets or blankets to protect the upholstery of your car.

ON TOP OF THE CAR

You can buy special roof-racks which fit on top of cars to carry bikes. On some the bikes are carried upside down, others the right way up; on others the right way up with the front wheel removed.

The advantages of this system are that the bikes are kept separate one from another (ie they do not rub against each other), you can get things out of the boot without problem and they do not obscure visibility.

The disadvantages are that you need to be reasonably tall and strong to lift bikes up on to the roof, it adds considerably to fuel consumption and feels somewhat precarious in strong crosswinds.

ON THE BACK OF THE CAR

This system seems to be the most versatile and popular method. Different racks can fit almost any sort of car with the use of clips, straps and adjustable angles.

The advantages of this system are that the rack itself folds down to a small space, the rack can be used on a variety of different cars, you do not need to be particularly tall or strong to load bikes on to the rack and fuel consumption is not as badly affected as by bikes on the top.

The disadvantages are that you may well need to buy a separate hang-on number plate and rear lighting system if the number plate, braking lights and indicators are obscured by the bikes; the bikes are pressed one against the other and may rub off paintwork; you will restrict access to the boot/hatchback.

The de-luxe system fits on to the back of a towbar, has its own lighting system and keeps the bikes separate as they fit into individual grooved rails. You can buy systems which hold two, three or four bikes.

Left: Thoroughly check all the straps when loading bikes.

GENERAL RULES ABOUT CARRYING BIKES

■ Remove all pumps, lights, panniers, water bottles and locks from the bikes before loading them on to the racks.

■ Lengths of pipe insulation material are useful for protecting the bikes from rubbing against each other. Try to avoid having delicate parts such as gear mechanisms pushed up against the frame or spokes of the adjoining bike.

■ Tie all straps with proper knots. Bows are not good enough.

■ Use stretch rubber bungees for extra security, particularly to ensure that the bottom of the bikes is attached to the bumper if you are carrying the bikes on the back of the car.

■ If the number plate or brake lights and indicators are obscured you are legally obliged to hang a separate number plate and lights from the back of the bikes.

■ It is essential to check and double check all the fixings before setting off and to stop and check again during the course of the journey to ensure nothing has slipped or come loose.

■ If you are leaving the bikes on the car for any length of time, lock them to each other and to the rack. While on your ride, it is as well to remove the rack and to lock it inside your car.

Top: The author on a research trip!

BIKES ON TRAINS

The regulations for carrying bikes on trains seem to change each year and vary from one operator to another, one sort of train to another and according to different times of the day and different days of the week. The only advice that can possibly be given that will remain useful is to take nothing for granted and ALWAYS phone before turning up at the station, to find out charges and availability of bike space. Even then you may find that incorrect information is given out: it is always best to go to the station and talk in person to the railway station staff.

Since privatisation different companies have adopted different approaches to carrying bikes on trains. The first step is to call the central number 0345 484950 and ask them if there are any restrictions on bikes on the train which you want to catch, ie how many bikes are allowed on the train, is there a charge and does the space need to be booked in advance?

Above: Trains allow quick exits from the city.

Dappled summer sunlight in the forest.

🚲 **ROUTE 1**

NORTH WIRRAL COASTAL PARK

A time will come when there will be an unbroken, top-quality cyclepath around the edge of the Wirral, from the Seacombe Ferry Terminal round to Hoylake, Heswall and Neston. Until that time we should enjoy the first stretch that is open and ready, from the ferry terminal through New Brighton to Meols on the eastern edge of Hoylake. It is an open, breezy ride that starts with wonderful views across the Mersey with the famous ferry plying its trade between Seacombe and the Royal Liver Buildings. Further north on the other side of the Mersey is the Port of Liverpool with hundreds of cranes loading and unloading containers. After passing through the Victorian resort of New Brighton the path runs alongside a golf course with big open skies and the vast expanse of Liverpool Bay to the north. The trail known as the North Wirral Coastal Park ends at Meols but if you want to extend the ride it is possible to link up with the Wirral Way (Ride 2) in West Kirby by using roads through Hoylake for about 3 miles.

New Brighton
The seaside town was established in the 1830s by James Atherton who hoped that it would come to outrank the resort of Brighton on the south coast. In Victorian times there was even a tower higher than the one at Blackpool.

North Wirral Coastal Park
The coast is well known for its wildlife, especially wading birds which visit during their migration — oystercatcher, dunlin, redshank and turnstone, for example. Leasowe Lighthouse was built in 1763 as one of several beacons used to guide ships safely into the Mersey Estuary.

Above Right: Well-maintained cyclepath alongside Liverpool bay.

Above: There will eventually be a cycle path right round the Wirral.

ROUTE 1
NORTH WIRRAL COASTAL PARK, LIVERPOOL

Starting Points: 1. Dove Point on Meols Parade, the coastal road on the eastern edge of Hoylake, by a sign which says 'No unauthorised vehicles'.
2. The Seacombe Ferry Terminal on the west side of the Mersey.

Parking: No cars are allowed along the promenade between the ferry terminal and New Brighton. There is parking in the side streets or at New Brighton.

Distance: 8 miles one way, 16 miles return.

Map: Ordnance Survey Landranger Sheet 108.

Hills: There are no hills.

Surface: All sealed surfaces.

Roads and Road Crossings: Care should be taken in New Brighton where there are several roads to cross.

Refreshments: Lots of choice in New Brighton.

Top: The Town Hall, Birkenhead.

Right: Top-grade path along the coast.

ROUTE INSTRUCTIONS:
The route is easy to follow — it runs along the coastline for 8 miles — as long as you keep the water to your right as you start from the Seacombe Ferry Terminal you won't go too far wrong!
1. From the Seacombe Ferry Terminal follow the broad (traffic-free) road north with the River Mersey to your right.

2. The route goes through New Brighton, turning west and running along the cycleway on the pavement then continuing in the same direction with the golf course to your left. This section through New Brighton is at present being improved so please follow the cycle signs directing you through to the North Wirral Coastal Park.

3. Follow this traffic-free route for 5 miles. It stops at Dove Point near Meols Parade, on the eastern edge of Hoylake.

 ROUTE 2

THE WIRRAL WAY FROM HOOTON STATION TO WEST KIRBY

Improvements are happening at a rapid pace on this 12-mile railway path along the west side of the Wirral. At present, large parts are divided into two sections: one for walkers and the other for horse riders and cyclists. This can become very confusing as the paths occasionally change sides and vary considerably in quality. Always show courtesy to other path users and if by any chance you find yourself on the walkers' side, slow right down and keep smiling! The improvement has started at the southern end of the path, from Hooton station, and so far reaches as far as Neston. The improvements have created a far better surface on the path as it runs through broadleaf woodland and banks of wild flowers; as you proceed north, there are views of the Dee Estuary to the west. On the outskirts of Neston you will pass through an amazing rock cutting where you feel as though Indiana Jones might suddenly swing across the path on a hanging creeper!

This Spread: Looking across the Dee Estuary to Wales

BACKGROUND AND PLACES OF INTEREST

History of the Railway Line

Wirral Country Park is based on the former 12-mile Hooton to West Kirby branch line railway. It opened in 1866 and ran for 90 years carrying freight and passengers and for a further six carrying just freight. The dismantled railway became Britain's first country park in the late 1960s. The most important remaining feature of railway days is the station at Hadlow Road, Willaston, which still looks as it might have done in the 1950s.

Starting Point and Parking: Hooton railway station car park (Park-and-Ride car park), to the northwest of Ellesmere Port and just west of the M53 Jct 5. Follow the A41 towards Chester then take the first right on to the B5133.

Distance: 12 miles one way, 24 miles return. The southern section is of a much higher quality so you may wish to shorten the ride considerably.

Maps: Ordnance Survey Landranger Sheets 108 and 117.

Hills: There are no hills.

Surface: A mixture of good quality gravel tracks and some rougher sections, likely to be muddy in winter and after prolonged rain. There is an ongoing project to improve the surface along the Wirral Way's whole length. As explained in the introduction there are occasionally parallel paths, one for walkers and one for other users. As these change sides from time to time you may find yourself on the walkers' side. Show courtesy, keep your speed down, warn people of your approach and thank them if they step aside for you.

Roads and Road Crossings: There are a couple of short road sections where the course of the railway line has been built over. Several road crossings, none of them very busy.

Refreshments: Coach & Horses PH, Neston. Lots of choice just off the route in Heswall. Refreshments at Thurstaston Visitor Centre. Lots of choice in West Kirby.

ROUTE INSTRUCTIONS:
The route is well signposted.

1. Exit the Hooton station car park, cross the railway line via the road bridge then turn immediately left to descend to the Wirral Way, at first running parallel with the railway line on a fairly narrow track.

2. The track widens and the surface improves after the first bridge. (Much of the Wirral Way will be brought up to this standard over the next few years, as time and money allow.) The Wirral Way briefly joins a lane then bears right on to a continuation of the trail, at first parallel with the lane.

3. Pass through an amazing rock cutting. At the crossroads with the road (Bushell Road to the right, Mellock Lane to the left, Station Road ahead) continue straight on, signposted 'Wirral Way'. Continue in the same direction. At the mini-roundabout at the end of Station Road turn left then on a sharp left-hand bend turn right. (It is better to cross the road before the bend.) Climb to rejoin the course of the railway path.

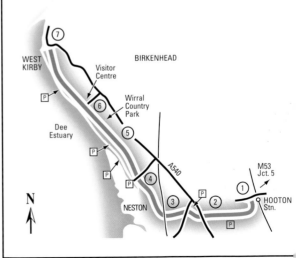

ROUTE 2
WIRRAL WAY, LIVERPOOL

4. At the junction with the next road (Neston Cricket Club is to your left) turn right then second left, signposted 'Wirral Way'.

5. Views of the Dee Estuary open up to the left. Three miles after Neston Cricket Club, at the T-junction with the road, turn right along Riverbank Road/Davenport Road which are quiet residential roads with new houses. After ¹/₂ mile bear right to rejoin the railway path.

6. After 2 miles go past Thurstaston Visitor Centre.

7. The Wirral Way ends after a further 3 miles at the busy A540 in West Kirby.

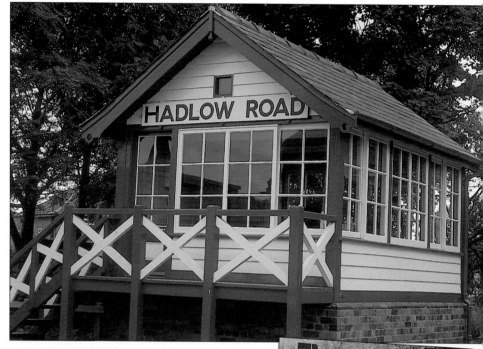

Top and Left: The old Hadlow Road Railway Station.

Above: Wirral Country Park is a linear park along the old railway line.

OTTERSPOOL PROMENADE, LIVERPOOL

The regeneration of Albert Dock has been the driving force behind the improvement along the whole length of the River Mersey from Cressington and Otterspool to the Royal Liver Buildings. A broad, top-grade promenade now sweeps alongside the river for 5 miles with wide open views across the water to the Wirral. The path is popular with walkers, joggers and cyclists but is wide enough to accommodate all three without trouble. Albert Dock houses the Beatles Museum amongst other attractions and offers a model of what can be done in terms of inner-city regeneration. If you are feeling fit and also want to enjoy the quintessential Liverpool experience, why not take the ferry across the Mersey and try out Ride 1, following the opposite bank of the river along the promenade to New Brighton and round the coast of the Wirral to Hoylake?

BACKGROUND AND PLACES OF INTEREST

Albert Dock

Opened in 1846 as England's gateway to the New World, Albert Dock is the largest group of Grade 1 listed buildings in Great Britain. It fell into disuse but has now been revamped into a quayside complex featuring watersports and museums. Alongside Animation World, The Beatles Story, the Tate Gallery and the Maritime Museum are a number of speciality shops and restaurants.

Starting Points and Parking: 1. The Royal Liver Buildings, in the centre of Liverpool. 2. The south end of the Otterspool Promenade. Turn off the A561 just west of Cressington station down Riversdale Road, following signs for 'Liverpool Cricket Ground'. There is a car park at the end. Descend to the riverside promenade and turn right.

Distance: 5 miles one way, 10 miles return.

Map: Ordnance Survey Landranger Sheet 108.

Hills: There are no hills.

Surface: All paved, occasionally cobbled.

Roads and Road Crossings: None.

Refreshments: Lots of choice in Albert Dock.

ROUTE INSTRUCTIONS:
It is hard to lose something as large as the River Mersey in Liverpool! Stay close to the water and you won't go far wrong. There are one or two short diversions away from the promenade but you soon return to the water's edge. The trail ends at the Royal Liver Buildings but from here you could easily catch a ferry to Seacombe on the other side and continue north along the traffic-free promenade that runs to New Brighton and around the coastline of the Wirral to Hoylake.

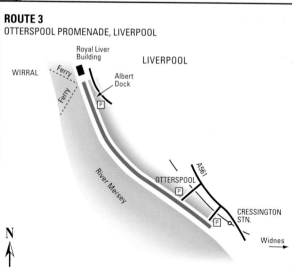

ROUTE 3
OTTERSPOOL PROMENADE, LIVERPOOL

Top: Albert Dock in Liverpool.

Above: Cycling towards Otterspool Promenade.

ST HELENS CANAL, FROM WIDNES TO WARRINGTON

Several rides in this book use sections of the Trans-Pennine Trail, the path for walkers and cyclists that crosses the country from Southport on the west coast to Hull and the North Sea coast, officially open at the end of 2000. The ride along St Helens Canal is the westernmost section included in the book although it is worth mentioning two nearby traffic-free paths to the north of Liverpool that are also on the Trans-Pennine Trail: the Liverpool Loop Line from Halewood to Aintree and the Cheshire Lines Path from Maghull to Ainsdale. This ride along St Helens Canal is surprisingly green, quiet and secluded for a setting so much in the heart of the industrial area between Liverpool and Manchester. Do not be surprised to see herons and even kingfishers along this stretch of water. The pub at Fiddler's Ferry offers a welcome refreshment stop and is a good turnaround point for an 8-mile ride. If you want to extend the ride you can easily follow the Trans-Pennine Trail signposts through Warrington on a mixture of tracks and quiet streets to join Route 5, the railway path from Warrington to Altrincham.

BACKGROUND AND PLACES OF INTEREST

Spike Island
The area was the birthplace of the British chemical industry and the Catalyst Museum explains the industry's history with photographs, slide shows and working machines. Since 1975 the area has been transformed into a green space and haven for wildlife.

Below: There is lots of wildlife along the canal.

Inset: Sustrans Millennium Milepost.

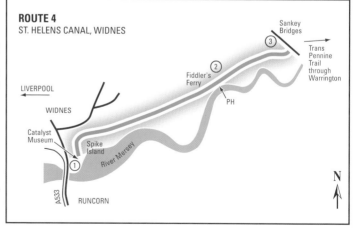

Starting Point and Parking:
The Catalyst Museum car park in Widnes (follow the brown and white signs from the A562/A533/A557).

Distance: 5¹/₂ miles one way, 11 miles return.

Map: Ordnance Survey Landranger Sheet 108.

Hills: There are no hills.

Surface: Good quality gravel tracks, some sections may become overgrown in summer.

Roads and Road Crossings: None.

Refreshments: Ferry Tavern at Fiddler's Ferry.

ROUTE INSTRUCTIONS:
1. From the corner of the Catalyst Museum car park by the path leading to the museum entrance bear left towards the locks. Cross the narrow bridge and turn left alongside the canal.

2. After 4 miles you will go past the Ferry Tavern.

3. The towpath ends after a further 1¹/₂ miles. It is possible to continue eastwards on the Trans-Pennine Trail by following signposts through Warrington on quiet roads and sections alongside the River Mersey and the Manchester Ship Canal to join the next long traffic-free section which runs along a railway path from Warrington through Lymm to the outskirts of Altrincham — see Route 5.

Top Right: Cooling towers across St Helens Canal.

Inset: The towpath offers fine cycling along a green corridor.

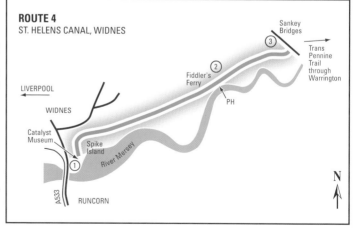

ROUTE 4
ST. HELENS CANAL, WIDNES

Sankey Bridges

Trans Pennine Trail through Warrington

③

②

Fiddler's Ferry

PH

LIVERPOOL

WIDNES

Catalyst Museum

Spike Island

River Mersey

①

A533

RUNCORN

N

ROUTE 5

WARRINGTON TO ALTRINCHAM ALONG THE TRANS-PENNINE TRAIL

There is a signboard at the western end of this trail, at the bottom of the approach ramp on the outskirts of Warrington, that places this short ride within a much wider context: not only is Warrington to Altrincham part of the much longer Trans-Pennine Trail stretching from coast to coast but the Trans-Pennine Trail itself is part of the European Long-Distance Footpath system which links such far-flung places as Geneva, Istanbul, St Petersburg and Riga! Finding the car park and the start of the ride on the west side of Altrincham will probably represent the hardest part of the day. Once on the trail it is impossible to get lost and the top-grade surface enables you to bowl along through open countryside and woodland with verges full of wild flowers in the late spring and early summer. This is a good ride for conversation — no hills and a wide track with good visibility — so that you can put the world to rights while keeping yourself fit! It would be easy to extend this ride westwards by following the Trans-Pennine Trail signs through Warrington to join the ride along St Helens Canal to Widnes (Route 4).

BACKGROUND AND PLACES OF INTEREST

History of the Railway
Passenger services along the Broadheath to Warrington rail line were axed by Beeching in 1965 but freight traffic continued until 1985. Trafford Metropolitan Borough Council bought the Broadheath to Heatley section in 1996. Money from English Partnerships has turned it into a recreational route.

The Red Rose Forest
One of 12 Community Forests in England, this partnership of Countryside Commission, Forestry Commission, local government and local people aims to create a well-wooded landscape across 292 square miles of Greater Manchester. It will make a greener and more pleasant setting for the forest's 1.5 million population to live, work and play in.

Starting Points and Parking:
1. Altrincham. (Grid Reference 751889.) From the M6 or the M56 follow the A556 north towards Altrincham. Go past the left turn to Dunham Massey (B5160) then after ¹/₂ mile, on a sharp right-hand bend, take the second of two closely-spaced left turns on to Highgate Road. This becomes Gorsey Lane. At the T-junction (mini-roundabout) turn left on to Oldfield Road (which becomes Seamons Road). Cross the bridge over the canal (traffic lights) then 150yds after passing the Bay Malton PH turn left into the car park. Beware the height barrier!
2. Bradshaw Lane, on the southeast edge of Warrington, just north of the junction of the A50 and the A56. (Grid Reference 638871).

Distance: 8 miles one way, 16 miles return. There are several pubs on or close to the route which would make good turnaround points if you wish to shorten the ride.

Map: Ordnance Survey Landranger Sheet 109.

Hills: There are no hills.

Surface: Good quality gravel track.

Roads and Road Crossings: Several quiet lanes to cross.

Refreshments: Bay Malton PH, west of Altrincham (near the start); The Balmoral at Lymm Hotel; Railway Inn, Dunham Woodhouses.

ROUTE INSTRUCTIONS: The route is well signposted and easy to follow. If you are travelling from east to west the M6 is about 6 miles along the trail (three-quarters of the total distance from Altrincham to Warrington).

Right: Locks on the Manchester Ship Canal in Warrington.

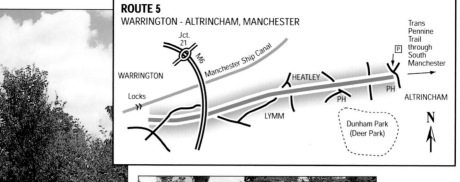

ROUTE 5
WARRINGTON - ALTRINCHAM, MANCHESTER

Jct. 21
M6
WARRINGTON
Manchester Ship Canal
Locks »
HEATLEY
LYMM
PH
PH
Dunham Park (Deer Park)
Trans Pennine Trail through South Manchester
P
ALTRINCHAM
N

Left: Easy cycling for children along the railway path.

Far Left: There are plenty of wild flowers in the woodland verges.

🚲 ROUTE 6

SALE WATER PARK, SOUTH MANCHESTER

Moving east along the Trans-Pennine Trail from Liverpool through Widnes, Warrington and Altrincham, this route alongside the River Mersey through Sale Water Park not only offers an existing ride alongside the river and around Chorlton Water but promises much more in the future when the quality of the riverside path is improved to the east and safe links are made to join this ride to the Warrington to Altrincham ride further west (Route 5). In the meantime, enjoy the open green spaces alongside the River Mersey with its profusion of wild flowers and birdlife.

Chorlton Water Park
Occupying the site of the old Barlow Hall Farm, 170-acre Chorlton Water Park is now one of the most popular sites in the Mersey Valley. Like Sale Water Park a kilometre downstream, the lake at Chorlton was excavated in the early 1970s to provide gravel for the M60 motorway. Since then the area has been developed to cater for all kinds of recreational activities in a countryside setting. During the winter months the lake is visited by large numbers of ducks including pochard, tufted duck and goldeneye.

Far Right: Taking mum out for a weekend ride.

Below: The River Mersey through Sale Water Park.

Right: There are paths on both sides of the River Mersey.

Starting Point and Parking: The Visitor Centre at Sale Water Park (Trafford Watersports Centre) off the M60 Jct 8.

Distance: (a) west from the Visitor Centre 1 mile one way, 2 miles return. (b) east from the Visitor Centre 2¹/₂ miles one way, 5 miles return.

Map/leaflet: Ordnance Survey Landranger Sheet 109. There are also several leaflets available from the Sale Water Park Visitor Centre.

Hills: There are no hills.

Surface: Gravel tracks on both sides of the River Mersey. Some of these are a bit rough, particularly further east, but as the Trans-Pennine Trail is developed it is highly likely that the surface will improve year by year.

Roads and Road Crossings: None

Refreshments: Café adjacent to the Visitor Centre; Jackson's Boat Inn at Jackson's Bridge.

ROUTE INSTRUCTIONS:
(Both routes) With your back to the entrance to the Visitor Centre go straight ahead on the narrow path running parallel with the road. Continue in the same direction to join the River Mersey by a sluice control building (remember this point for your return). At this point you have a choice:
1. (To the west). Turn left on the track alongside the river. Follow this for 1 mile as far as the railway line and the next bridge over the river. From this point you can return on the higher or lower track. There is also a track on the other side of the river but it is rougher. Return to the sluice control building.

2. (To the east). Turn right along the river then cross the bridge over the river (by Jackson's Boat PH) and turn right. After 1 mile, opposite a metal bridge with anti-climbing barbs, go through a barrier and turn left down to Chorlton Water Park. Complete a circuit of the lake, return to this point

on the River Mersey then go back to the Visitor Centre.

There are tracks on both sides of the river but parts are quite rough. This is likely to improve when the Trans-Pennine Trail is fully open.

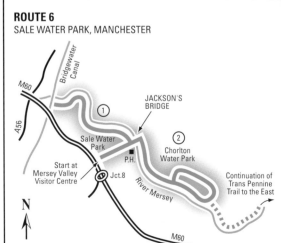

ROUTE 6
SALE WATER PARK, MANCHESTER

DELAMERE FOREST, CHESHIRE
(9 miles east of Chester)

There are very few Forestry Commission holdings of any size in the area covered by this book — you would need to go to Wales or Yorkshire for that — but whilst Delamere Forest Park is not particularly large, it does have two waymarked cycle routes which are ideal for family cycling with broad gravel tracks. There are a few gentle hills but nothing to really worry about. Starting from the Visitor Centre the ride crosses and recrosses the railway line, passing through mixed broadleaf and conifer woodland, with a fine display of wild flowers in the spring and early summer. You have to twice cross a road running east-west through the forest. Although it is marked as a minor road on the map, it can at times be quite busy and the traffic can be travelling fast so take great care on both crossings.

BACKGROUND AND PLACES OF INTEREST

Delamere Forest
The woodlands were once the royal hunting preserve of the Earls of Chester — the Visitor Centre has displays of Delamere's history. The forest is noted for kestrels, sparrowhawks, foxes and badgers.

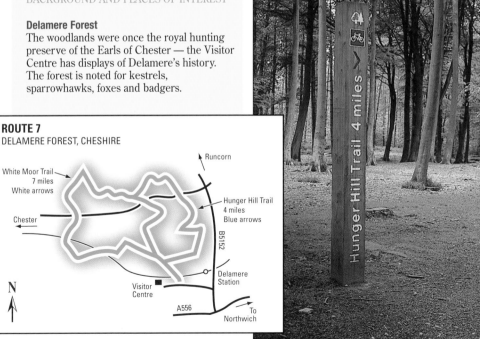

ROUTE 7
DELAMERE FOREST, CHESHIRE

Runcorn

White Moor Trail
7 miles
White arrows

Hunger Hill Trail
4 miles
Blue arrows

Chester

B5152

Delamere
Station

Visitor
Centre

A556

To
Northwich

N

Hatch Mere in Delamere Forest

The well-waymarked Hunger Hill Trail.

Starting Point and Parking: The car park by the Visitor Centre in Delamere Forest is situated just off the B5152, close to Delamere railway station, 7 miles south of Runcorn and 9 miles east of Chester.

Distance: (a) the Hunger Hill Trail, 4 miles, blue arrows. (b) the White Moor Trail, 7 miles, white arrows.

Map: Ordnance Survey Landranger Sheet 117.

Hills: Several gentle hills.

Surface: Good quality stone tracks.

Roads and Road Crossings: Care should be taken crossing the public road that cuts through the forest. Although marked as a minor road, the traffic can be travelling fast along it.

Refreshments: There is a café at the old station just by the main road.

Cycle Hire: At the Visitor Centre (01625 572681).

ROUTE INSTRUCTIONS:
The two routes are well signposted.
1. From the car park by the Delamere Forest Visitor Centre return towards the public road and take the first left over a bridge with a 'No entry' (for cars) signpost. You will come to an obvious crossroads of tracks where you have a choice:

(a) the Hunger Hill Trail, 4 miles, blue arrows, to the right;

(b) the White Moor Trail, 7 miles, white arrows, to the left.

Below: Father and son in the forest.

🚲 ROUTE 8

WHITEGATE WAY, CHESHIRE
(12 miles east of Chester)

There aren't many cycle trails in the country that end at a salt mine, as the Whitegate Trail does just to the north of Winsford. The railway path is predominantly wooded through the cuttings, with views across to arable farmland and pasture on the more open sections and embankments. As with so many of these railway paths the Whitegate Way is at its best either in late spring/early summer when the young leaves are a fresh green and the verges and woodland are full of bright wild flowers, or in late autumn when the leaves are changing colour and the path is carpeted with all shades of yellow and red. Some sections of this route are not that well drained so in winter and after rain you may well encounter several muddy sections.

BACKGROUND AND PLACES OF INTEREST

History of the Railway
The Whitegate Line was opened in 1870 to transport salt from the mines and works along the west bank of the River Weaver. The line closed in 1966. The old railway is now managed for the maximum benefit of wildlife as well as providing an attractive environment for people to enjoy. Trees are coppiced in a traditional form of woodland management whereby the trees are cut down to ground level every 6-8 years. This encourages tremendous regrowth and provides useful timber for poles and logs.

Below: The narrow railway path through the woodland.

Starting Point and Parking: The car park for the Whitegate Way is at Marton Green, to the north of the A54 between Kelsall and Winsford. Turn on to Clay Lane, opposite a lane signposted 'Budworth'. After 1 mile, just before a railway bridge, bear right downhill signposted 'Whitegate Way' for the car park. (Grid Reference 615680.)

Distance: It is 3 miles one way, 6 miles return if you turn right (east) from the car park; and 4 miles one way, 8 miles return if you turn left (west) to Cuddington.

Maps: Ordnance Survey Landranger Sheets 117 and 118.

Hills: There are no hills.

Surface: Reasonable gravel track with several muddy sections, particularly in the winter and after rain.

Roads and Road Crossings: None, unless you decide to go to the pub in Cuddington.

Refreshments: Pub in Cuddington.

ROUTE INSTRUCTIONS:
The route follows the course of the old railway so it is impossible to get lost! From the car park you can:
1. Head east (turn right) for 3 miles until you reach the T-junction with the road by the salt mines.

2. Head west (turn left) for 4 miles until you come to a huge railway bridge over the trail by Ravenscough in Cuddington.

ROUTE 8
WHITEGATE WAY, CHESHIRE

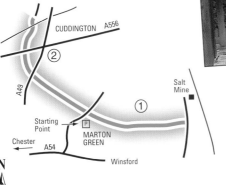

Top: Tunnel beneath the railway near Cuddington.

Above: The old Whitegate Railway Station signboard.

THE TRANS-PENNINE TRAIL NEAR PENISTONE
(7 miles west of Barnsley)

The Trans-Pennine Trail crosses the Pennines between Longdendale and Dunford Bridge, passing above the Woodhead Tunnels which used to carry the railway line. So from Dunford Bridge (at 300m/985ft) down to the end of the ride at the River Don south of Thurgoland (at 150m/490ft) there is a drop of 500ft over almost 12 miles. Take into account the likelihood of the wind blowing from the west and you soon see that it is normally a lot quicker heading east downhill with the wind behind you than heading west uphill into the wind! Penistone is an attractive stone-built town with plenty of choices of refreshment. Heading west from here the views are of dry-stone walls and sheep-grazed moorland in the Upper Don Valley. There is a welcome pub at Dunford Bridge, the turnaround point. To the east of Penistone the trail is increasingly wooded as it drops in height. The ride could easily be linked either to Ride 10, The Dove Valley Trail, by following the Trans-Pennine Trail signs from Oxspring to Silkstone Common or alternatively to Ride 12, Wharncliffe Wood, by joining the forestry track just south of the A616.

BACKGROUND AND PLACES OF INTEREST

Penistone
A busy market town with a 13th-century church. The Cloth Hall and Shambles date from the late 18th century.

Below: There is a gentle downhill from Dunford Bridge to Oxspring.

Starting Point and Parking: Penistone lies 7 miles west of Barnsley on the A628 (west of M1 Jct 37). Follow signs for the free car park in Penistone (just south of the main part of the village, near to the fire station).

Distance: (a) Penistone to Dunford Bridge — 6 miles one way, 12 miles return. (b) Penistone to Wharncliffe Crags — 6 miles one way, 12 miles return.

Map: Ordnance Survey Landranger Sheet 110.

Hills: There is a steady climb from Penistone to Dunford Bridge and a steady descent in the other direction, ie it will be easier cycling east than cycling west!

Surface: Good quality gravel tracks.

Roads and Road Crossings: There are no dangerous crossings.

Refreshments: Pub at Dunford Bridge; lots of choice in Penistone; pub just off the route in Oxspring.

ROUTE INSTRUCTIONS:
The route is well signposted as the Trans-Pennine Trail or the Upper Don Trail. From the car park in Penistone follow the gravel track across the open land ahead and join the railway path. Either:
1.Turn left (west) for Dunford Bridge (6 miles, gentle 300ft climb);

2. Turn right (east) for Wharncliffe Wood (6 miles, gentle 200ft descent).

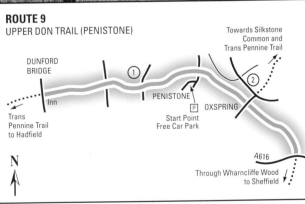

Above: Fork in the Trans-Pennine Trail near to Oxspring.

Top Left: Verge side wild flowers on the upper Don Trail.

Left: Stone sculpture marking the opening of the trail.

ROUTE 9
UPPER DON TRAIL (PENISTONE)

🚲 ROUTE 10

THE DOVE VALLEY TRAIL NEAR BARNSLEY
(2 miles south of Barnsley)

Passing through the rolling countryside to the south of Barnsley it is gratifying to see the enormous efforts that have been made to transform the ugly spoil heaps and wastelands of the coal mining industry into either green and wooded areas or into a wetlands nature reserve (the Old Moor Wetland Centre) with man-made lakes attracting a wide variety of wildfowl. There is a real case of nature being actively encouraged to heal over scars and one wonders whether any present inhabitant would recognise the place in 50 years' time when the trees have had a chance to mature and the hard edges of the massive earth moving exercises have been softened by the growth of grass and wild flowers. Barnsley is the headquarters of the Trans-Pennine Trail and in addition to the Dove Valley Trail (which is part of the Trans-Pennine Trail) there are also links right into Barnsley and plans for a route parallel with the Dove Valley Trail known as the Timberland Trail.

BACKGROUND AND PLACES OF INTEREST

History of the Railway
The Worsbrough Bank Railway was opened in 1880 to allow large amounts of Lancashire-bound coal traffic to bypass the serious bottleneck of Barnsley. The Bank included $2^1/_2$ miles of 1 in 40 gradient, one of the steepest gradients in the country and a severe obstacle to heavily-laden westbound coal trains. In 1952 the line was electrified, one of the first such schemes in Britain. The 142-minute journey from Wath to Dunford Bridge was whittled down to 66 minutes! The track was closed in 1981.

Main Picture: Along the Dove Valley Trail near Silkstone Common.

Inset: The Trans-Pennine Trail comprises many railway sections.

Starting Point and Parking: There is a Pay and Display car park at Worsbrough Mill Country Park, 3 miles north of Jct 36 of the M1, along the A61 towards Barnsley. The Trans-Pennine Trail crosses the A61 about 200yds north of the exit to the car park.

Distance: Worsbrough Country Park to Silkstone Common — 4 miles one way, 8 miles return. Worsbrough Country Park to Old Moor Wetland Centre — 6 miles one way, 12 miles return.

Maps: Ordnance Survey Landranger Sheets 110 and 111.

Hills: Gentle 170ft climb west to Silkstone Common. Gentle 100ft descent east to the Old Moor Wetland Centre.

Surface: Good quality gravel tracks.

Roads and Road Crossings: You will probably prefer to use the pavement for 200yds from the car park at Worsbrough Mill to the point where the Trans-Pennine Trail crosses the A61. Heading east, care should be taken crossing the B6100 in Worsbrough, close to the start of the ride.

Refreshments: Pub at Silkstone Common; refreshments just off the route in Wombwell.

ROUTE INSTRUCTIONS:
The route is well signposted as the Trans-Pennine Trail or the Dove Valley Trail. Exit Worsbrough Country Park car park and turn left along the main A61 (push your bike along the pavement for 200yd).
1. (Route west to Silkstone Common). Turn left off the A61 on to the old railway path and climb gently for 4 miles, crossing the M1. The railway path ends at the southern edge of Silkstone Common (just before the old tunnel). Here you have a choice of turning round and making your way straight back to Worsbrough, going into Silkstone Common

for refreshments or of following the Trans-Pennine Trail further west on a mixture of rougher tracks and minor roads to join the next railway section from Oxspring to Penistone and Dunford Bridge (see Route 9).

2. (Route east to the Old Moor Wetland Centre). Cross the A61 with care on to the railway path leading east signposted 'Public Bridleway'. After 1¹⁄₂ miles pass beneath a railway viaduct then keep bearing right to cross two bridges over the A633. A track from Barnsley joins from the left (remember this point for your return). Go past a Go Kart circuit, Wombwell FC ground and a Thomas the Tank Engine model. Cross into the Old Moor Wetland Centre and complete a circuit of the lake. Return to Worsbrough Country Park.

ROUTE 10
DOVE VALLEY TRAIL, BARNSLEY

SILKSTONE COMMON

PH

Dove Valley Trail

Trans Pennine Trail to Penistone

Worsbrough Mill Country Park

Start Point

A61

M1

A633
To Barnsley

WOMBWELL

Nature Reserve

Trans Pennine Trail to Doncaster

N

Above: Taking a well-earned break.

Right: Looking towards the Nature Reserve near Wombwell.

THE TRANS-PENNINE TRAIL FROM DONCASTER TO THE EARTH CENTRE AND HARLINGTON

The Earth Centre is a visionary exhibition centre created amid the wasteland left over from decades of mining. It has acted as a catalyst to regenerate the whole of the surrounding area, greening the spoil heaps and showing how the future can take greater account of renewable sources of energy and make better use of recycling the world's dwindling resources. The ride starts on the outskirts of Doncaster (in the future there will be a much safer cycle route right from the heart of Doncaster to this point) and follows the course of a dismantled railway to the first viaduct over the river. There is a lovely stretch along the wooded banks of the River Don through the attractions of Sprotbrough and up a steep climb to the second viaduct. The trail leads right past the Earth Centre and along the valley of the River Dearne to Harlington. In the future there will be a traffic-free trail all the way to Barnsley.

BACKGROUND AND PLACES OF INTEREST

The Don Valley
The River Don was once a major route for transporting goods across the country. Water traffic still uses the River Don near Sprotbrough. The valley has a richly interwoven industrial and ecological heritage. Sprotbrough Flash, an expanse of open water, was created by subsidence from coalmining at Cadeby and Denaby Main. It sustains overwintering birds such as the little grebe, mute swan and tufted duck. The great crested grebe returned to the Flash in the 1950s after an absence of almost 100 years. Sir Walter Scott worked on his novel Ivanhoe whilst staying at the Boat Inn in Sprotbrough.

Main Picture: The railway viaduct east of Conisbrough.

Above Right: Travelling light on a summer's day.

Right: Barges are moored near Sprotborough.

Starting Point and Parking: The shopping area by B&Q on the A638 to the northwest of Doncaster. Parking is available in the side streets or ask for permission to use the car parks belonging to the shops.

Distance: 8 miles one way, 16 miles return. For a shorter ride, the Boat Inn at Sprotbrough (6 mile round trip) or the Earth Centre (12 mile round trip) make good turnaround points.

Map: Ordnance Survey Landranger Sheet 111.

Hills: There are several gentle hills and two steeper ones to climb from the riverside up on to the massive railway viaducts over the River Don.

Surface: Good quality gravel tracks.

Roads and Road Crossings: One road to cross (near Dearne Bridge). There is a short section on road if you wish to visit the pub in Harlington.

Refreshments: The Boat Inn, Sprotbrough; café at the Earth Centre (you will have to pay the entrance fee to go in); the Harlington Inn, Harlington.

ROUTE INSTRUCTIONS:
The route is well signposted as the Trans-Pennine Trail.
1. From the car park by B&Q, return to the main road, turn left (away from Doncaster) down to the cyclepath and turn left again signposted 'Sprotbrough, Cusworth Cycle Route'. Follow this railway path for 2½ miles.

2. Just before the huge viaduct over the river descend steeply via the steps to the right (there are plans for a ramp in the future). Follow alongside the river for 3 miles, passing beneath the A1(M) road bridge, alongside the locks and the Boat Inn at Sprotbrough.

3. Continue along the broad stone track, climbing steeply to join the right-hand end of the tall viaduct ahead. Continue on the track past the Earth Centre.

4. At the road cross straight ahead then turn right over the wooden bridge and join a railway path. Follow this for 1½ miles. Opposite a footbridge over the river turn right onto a track.

5. This turns to tarmac. At the T-junction (at the end of Mill Lane) turn left as far as the Harlington Inn.

ROUTE 11
DONCASTER - EARTH CENTRE

Trans Pennine Trail to Selby

A638

HARLINGTON

Trans Pennine Trail to Barnsley

PH

Sprotbrough

A1(M)

DONCASTER

PH

Earth Centre

Tall viaduct over River Don

Second tall viaduct over River Don

Conisbrough

N

Far Left: A fine new bridge near the Earth Centre.

Above: Lovely woodland section south of Sprotbrough.

Inset: Newly-planted trees at the Earth Centre.

WHARNCLIFFE WOOD, NEAR SHEFFIELD

(5 miles northwest of Sheffield)

There are few large Forestry Commission woodlands in the area and even fewer with waymarked trails so Wharncliffe Wood, lying just north of Sheffield, is something of an exception. There are two trails waymarked, one described as difficult using narrow, twisting tracks, the other uses the broad forestry roads but also involves a long climb back to the start, as is inevitable with any ride that starts on top of a hill! If you are looking for a longer ride it would be quite feasible to drop down the hillside towards the bottom of the valley of the River Don on forestry tracks and head north along the railway path that leads north and west to Penistone and Dunford Bridge, all off-road and traffic-free (see Route 9.) Further afield, to the west of Sheffield, there are some superb traffic-free trails in the Upper Derwent Valley, covered more fully in the first volume of *Cycling Without Traffic: The Midlands & Peak District.*

BACKGROUND AND PLACES OF INTEREST

Wharncliffe and Grenoside Woods
The Wharncliffe and Grenoside area has been extensively used by man since the Iron Age, first as a base for hunting groups then later as a source of querns or hand mills for grinding grain. This gave rise to the original name 'Querncliff'. In the medieval period parts of the chase were enclosed as a deer park and in more recent times much mining and quarrying has taken place for coal, ganister and fire clay in Wharncliffe and building stone in Grenoside.

Top Right: Spring and early summer are the best times for wild flowers.

Below: Broad forest track through Wharncliffe Woods.

Inset: If only it were true for the bike ride — here you will finish with a hill.

Starting Point and Parking: There is a car park in the woods at the top of the hill, off the minor road that leads north from Grenoside to Wortley (Grid Reference 325950). (Five miles northwest of Sheffield.)

Distance: 3-mile circuit (or longer options on woodland tracks if you take a map with you).

Map: Ordnance Survey Landranger Sheet 110.

Hills: Long descent for the first half of the ride, long climb for the second half!

Surface: Good quality gravel tracks.

Roads and Road Crossings: None.

Refreshments: None en route, the closest are at Grenoside.

Route Instructions: The route is well signposted with green bike signs.
1. From the car park go through the metal barrier and continue downhill following black and green bike route waymarks. Ignore a left turn, take the next turning to the right.

2. Ignore the next left turning, continue on to a T-junction (Grid Reference 307947) turn left* and carry on downhill.

*For a longer route turn right here to explore the lower part of the forest. You will need Ordnance Survey Landranger Sheet 110 to help you find your way.

3. Ignore another left turn. At a major crossroads of tracks go straight ahead then shortly follow the main track round to the left.

4. Long climb. At the T-junction turn right on to the steepest climb of the day to return to the car park/start.

ROUTE 12
WHARNCLIFFE / GRENOSIDE WOODS, SHEFFIELD

ROUTE 13

ROTHER VALLEY COUNTRY PARK TO STAVELEY
(6 miles southeast of Sheffield)

With its craft centre, exhibitions, café, plentiful wildfowl plus a variety of rides and walks, Rother Valley Country Park is an ideal place to spend the day. A 3-mile circuit of the two lakes may be all the cycling that you want to do but if you are interested in a longer challenge then there is a dismantled railway on the western side of the lakes that runs 6 miles south from Beighton to Staveley through a mixture of wooded cuttings and open stretches with views out into the surrounding countryside. The ride forms part of both the Trans-Pennine Trail (the southern link from Chesterfield through Sheffield to Barnsley) and also Sustrans National Route 6 which runs north from Derby via Nottingham, Worksop, Sheffield and Doncaster to York. The two routes join at the southern end of the lake, so don't be confused if you see a mixture of 'Route 6', 'Route 67' and 'Trans-Pennine Trail' signs.

BACKGROUND AND PLACES OF INTEREST

Rother Valley Country Park
Set in 750 acres of countryside, the park offers an enormous range of leisure and recreational activities on both land and water. At the centre of the park stands a historic complex of buildings based around Bedgreave Mill, now the Visitor Centre. Bedgreave New Mill was built near the site of earlier mills and dates from the late 1700s. The restored mill houses an exhibition which depicts the history of the area and the buildings. Next to the Visitor Centre is a café and craft centre.

Below: Cycling keeps you ten years younger!

Starting Point and Parking: The car park at Rother Valley Country Park, 3 miles southwest of M1 Jct 31.

Distance: 3-mile circuit of the lake. A further 6 miles from Beighton to Staveley (ie 12 miles return).

Map: Ordnance Survey Landranger Sheet 120.

Hills: There are no hills.

Surface: Good quality gravel tracks.

Roads and Road Crossings: None.

Refreshments: Café at the Visitor Centre.

ROUTE INSTRUCTIONS:
The route is well signposted as the Trans-Pennine Trail, Route 6 or Route 67.
1. From the Rother Valley Country Park Visitor Centre make your way to the lakeside and turn right (ie keep the water to your left). Pass between the two lakes and continue alongside the water.

2. You could either continue the circuit of the lake for a 3-mile ride or for a link to the Trans-Pennine Trail, when you reach a point opposite the Sailing Club (on the other side of the water) and with a double metal gate and a wooden bridlegate across the path, turn right under the railway bridge then turn left on to the old railway path following signs for Killamarsh and Staveley.

3. Follow this trail for 5 miles, at one point passing through a small car park and following the Trans-Pennine Trail up to the left.

4. The easy trail ends at a point where a bridge with steps crosses a railway (just north of Staveley). It is suggested you turn around at this point* and return to the Visitor Centre, completing the circuit of the lake.

If you continue south along the Trans-Pennine Trail, a short rough section will take you to the Chesterfield Canal (Ride 14).

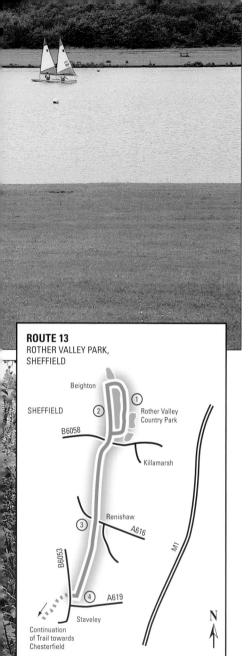

ROUTE 13
ROTHER VALLEY PARK,
SHEFFIELD

Beighton

SHEFFIELD

Rother Valley
Country Park

B6058

Killamarsh

Renishaw

A616

M1

B6053

A619

Staveley

Continuation
of Trail towards
Chesterfield

N

Top: Sailing on the lake in Rother Valley Country Park.

Left: Brightly coloured mallow on the side of the path.

CHESTERFIELD CANAL
(North of Chesterfield)

At the Tapton Lock Visitor Centre about one mile north of the start of the ride in Chesterfield you will come across a sign which indicates that following the canal south will lead to Chesterfield, whereas following it north will lead to Istanbul! The explanation is that the Chesterfield Canal towpath is part of the Southern Link of the Trans-Pennine Trail and the Trans-Pennine Trail itself is part of the much larger European Long-Distance Footpath system which extends as far as Turkey! I wouldn't recommend setting out from Chesterfield expecting to find signposts to Istanbul for the next 2,000 miles — one imagines that it will be another generation before all these visionary schemes are connected into a satisfyingly complete network. So... enjoy the 5 miles along the canal towpath taking you north away from the famous twisted spire of Chesterfield's church past old red-brick locks to its somewhat abrupt end on the western edges of Staveley.

BACKGROUND AND PLACES OF INTEREST

The Chesterfield Canal
A bold and imaginative product of the early years of the Industrial Revolution, the prime purpose of the Chesterfield Canal was to take Derbyshire's coal to new markets. The original surveys were done by the famous canal engineer, James Brindley, although he did not live to see its opening in 1777. For its time it was a magnificent piece of engineering, with the country's longest tunnel (at the time) at Norwood and one of the earliest examples of a large staircase of locks at Thorpe Salvin.

Tapton Lock
The route of the Chesterfield Canal follows the River Rother valley out of the town; Tapton Lock is the first of five carrying the canal down to Staveley. The lock was constructed in 1777 and is a typical narrow lock, 72ft long and 7ft wide. It fell into disuse, but was restored in the late 1980s. Each lock gate weighs approximately 1 ton and was manufactured from solid oak at the Rochdale Canal Workshops.

Below: The canal takes you from town to country.

Starting Point and Parking: The car park in the centre of Chesterfield near the Chesterfield Hotel and Chesterfield College (just west of the railway station). To get to the start of the canal, follow Brimington Road (B6543/A619) towards Tapton/Brimington/ Staveley, turn first left on to Holbeck Close then after 100yds, shortly after the Chesterfield Canal information board, bear right on to a narrow path.

Distance: 5 miles one way, 10 miles return.

Maps/leaflets: Ordnance Survey Landranger Sheets 119 and 120. Various leaflets about the canal can be obtained from the Tapton Lock Visitor Centre.

Hills: There are no hills.

Surface: Good quality gravel tracks, narrow at the start in the centre of Chesterfield.

Roads and Road Crossings: None.

Refreshments: Lots of choice in Chesterfield; limited refreshments at the Tapton Lock Visitor Centre.

ROUTE INSTRUCTIONS:
Once you have found the start in Chesterfield no instructions are needed as it is hard to lose a canal! The route ends where the canal ends, at the barrier on the western edge of Staveley (Grid Reference 430746). There are plans to improve the route north to connect with the dismantled railway path that leads on to Killamarsh, Beighton and Rother Valley Country Park (Route 13).

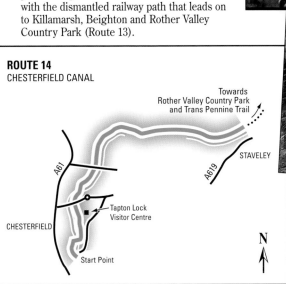

ROUTE 14
CHESTERFIELD CANAL

Towards
Rother Valley Country Park
and Trans Pennine Trail

STAVELEY

A61

A619

Tapton Lock
Visitor Centre

CHESTERFIELD

Start Point

N

Top: The crooked church spire in Chesterfield.

Above: An old red-brick bridge over the canal.

CLUMBER PARK TO CRESWELL CRAGS
(4 miles southeast of Worksop)

Creswell Crags are believed to be the most northerly point in Britain where humans and animals lived during the last Ice Age and there have been many archaeological discoveries backing up the theory. It is well worth leaving yourself time to explore the area on foot once you have cycled over from Clumber Park. There are a mixture of roads, good tracks through woodland and rougher or sandier tracks, including one leading down through an atmospheric rock cutting to cross the great estates from Clumber Park through Welbeck Park to Creswell Crags. Be warned that there are two busy roads to cross where great care should be taken as the traffic can be travelling quite fast. In addition, on the return the visibility is not brilliant. If in doubt, follow the road north or south until you are happy about your crossing point and walk back along the verge on the other side. This is particularly important if you are with children.

BACKGROUND AND PLACES OF INTEREST

Creswell Crags
More than 45,000 years ago Neanderthal Man hunted woolly rhinos and bison that lived in caves in these limestone crags. After them, 13,000 years ago, came the 'Creswellians' who created sophisticated tools and works of art. The Visitor Centre shows the history of the caves' inhabitants.

Main Picture: Cresswell Crags.

Inset: Bridleway between Clumber and Cresswell Crags.

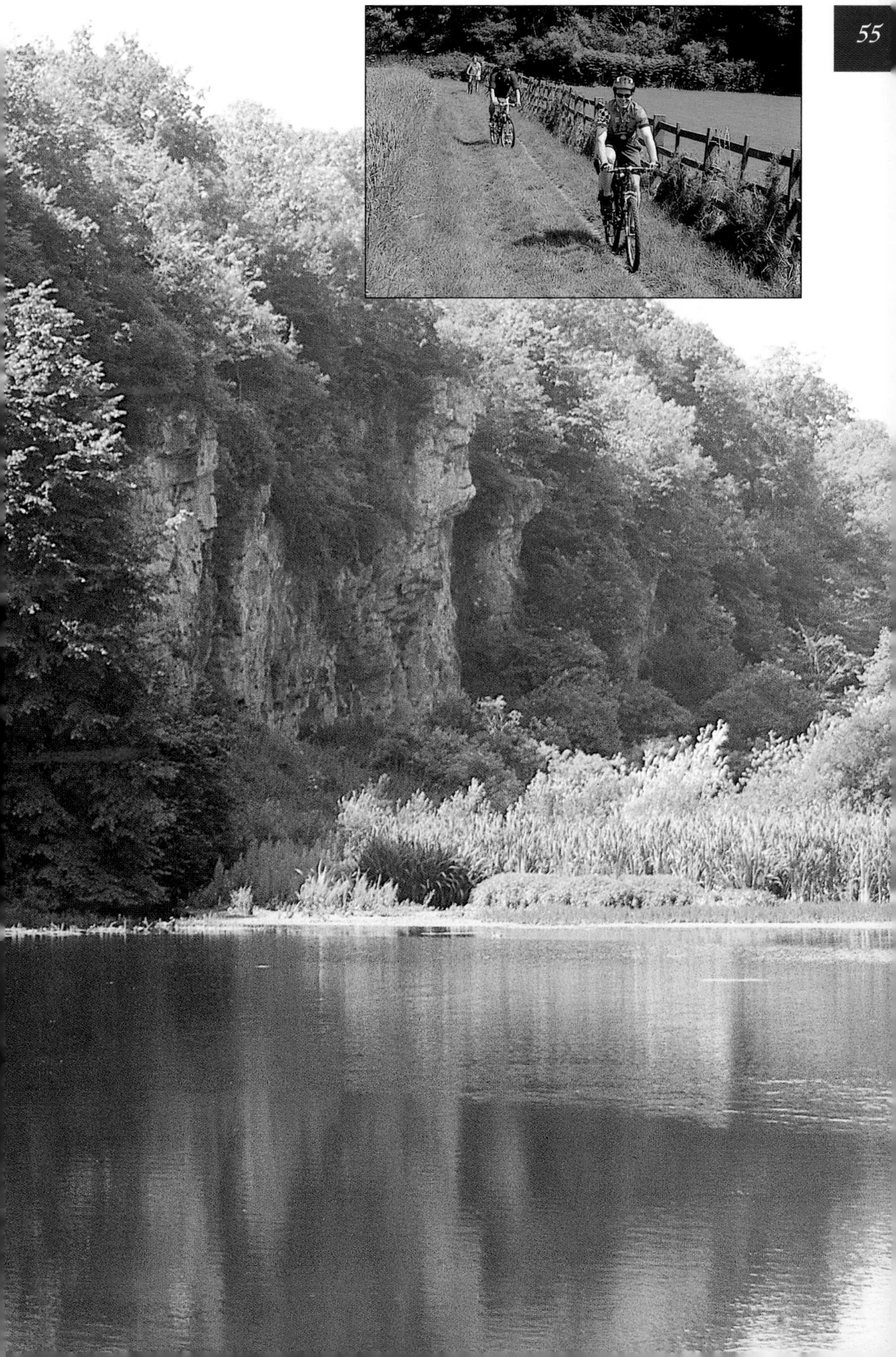

Starting Points and Parking: 1. The car park by the Cycle Hire Centre in Clumber Park, 4 miles southeast of Worksop. 2. The car park at Creswell Crags, off the B6042 southwest of Worksop.

Distance: 6¹/₂ miles one way, 13 miles return.

Map: Ordnance Survey Landranger Sheet 120.

Hills: There is a steady 200ft climb from the start to the highpoint of the Robin Hood Way to the west of the B6034. On the return there is a steep climb through a stone cutting to get back up to this point.

Surface: A wide variety of surfaces from tarmac to good gravel tracks, rougher tracks which may be muddy in winter and soft sandy conditions. Best to use mountain bikes. The ride is not suitable for very young children.

Roads and Road Crossings: Extreme care should be taken crossing both the B6034 and the A60, particularly on the return trip. Allow yourself time to gauge the speed of the traffic before crossing.

Refreshments: At the Visitor Centres at Clumber Park and Creswell Crags.

Cycle Hire: At Clumber Park (01909 476592 or 01909 484977).

ROUTE INSTRUCTIONS:
1. From the Cycle Hire Centre turn left then follow this road to the right. Follow Clumber Lane (some estate traffic) in the same direction for 2 miles.*

There are several other options to get from the Cycle Hire Centre to Truman's Lodge on forest tracks. Buy a map of the park and work out your preferred route (for example, if you follow the waymarked Red Bike Route clockwise you will get there).

2. 300yds after passing through Truman's Lodge bear left on to a track by a wooden barrier signposted 'Public Bridleway'. Shortly afterwards take great care crossing the busy B6034 on to the bridleway opposite.

3. Continue in the same direction passing remote stone buildings. Descend through an atmospheric rock cutting. At the next house (South Lodge) turn left and go through a gate and across a field, following 'Public Bridleway' signposts.

4. At the T-junction with tarmac turn right then shortly after passing a private road to the left take the next track left. At the next T-junction with a road turn right (remember this point for your return).

5. Go straight across at two crossroads with estate roads. With great care cross the A60 and continue straight ahead for ³/₄ mile to Creswell Crags Visitor Centre. Retrace your route, taking care at the two road crossings.

Left: A great weekend outing for friends and family.

Below: The deep stone cutting through woodland near Clumber.

Inset: It's never too early to start cycling.

ROUTE 15
CLUMBER PARK TO CRESWELL CRAGS

A CIRCUIT WITHIN CLUMBER PARK

(4 miles southeast of Worksop)

Clumber Park is likely to become one of the most popular destinations for recreational family cycling in the country, ranking alongside Rutland Water and the Peak District railway trails. This is due to the superb infrastructure of cycle hire with all sorts of bikes and trailers available, the excellent mix of quiet estate roads, broad gravel tracks through woodlands, waymarked circuits and the beautiful setting with the lake, famous old stone bridge and chapel. There is an excellent

Below: Taking a break after a circuit of Clumber Park.

Right: Clumber Chapel, across the lake.

Inset: Temple on the east side of Clumber Lake.

Visitor Centre and café and plenty of places to choose for a picnic or barbecue in the thousands of acres of parkland. It is also on the Sustrans National Route 6 which runs north from Derby to York and if you arrive by bike there is no entry fee to pay to get into the park!

BACKGROUND AND PLACES OF INTEREST

Clumber Park

A National Trust property of some 3,800 acres, Clumber House was demolished in 1938, a victim of economic decline and heavy taxation. The remains of the stableblock and the Duke's study now house the National Trust shop, restaurant and information room. Clumber Bridge was built in 1770 and the lake took 15 years to complete. Clumber Chapel was built in 1889 for the 7th Duke of Newcastle and is a fine example of Gothic Revival architecture, described as a 'cathedral in miniature'. Limetree Avenue, the longest such avenue in Europe, was planted by the 4th Duke in 1840.

Starting Point and Parking: The car park by the Cycle Hire Centre in Clumber Park, 4 miles southeast of Worksop.

Distance: 13-mile circuit.

Map/leaflet: Ordnance Survey Landranger Sheet 120. Better is the A4 map available from the Cycle Hire Centre or the more comprehensive map you can buy from the Visitor Centre.

Hills: There are several gentle hills.

Surface: A mixture of good quality gravel tracks and some rougher sections likely to be muddy in winter or after prolonged rain.

Roads and Road Crossings: Care should be taken crossing the estate roads although none of these are very busy.

Refreshments: At the Visitor Centre.

Cycle Hire: At the Cycle Hire Centre (01909 476592 or 01909 484977).

ROUTE INSTRUCTIONS:
The route is well signposted with red bike signs.
1. From the Cycle Hire Centre turn left then bear left, following red and green bike signs carefully. Shortly after crossing Clumber Bridge bear right on to the no through road signposted 'South Lodge'.

2. At the T-junction of tracks shortly after passing South Lodge, turn left and follow this track (muddy in winter) for 2 miles.

3. Easy to miss! When the main road (A614) is in earshot, immediately after a small round picnic table, turn left on to a track by a low wooden post. At a crossroads with an estate road (stone pillars to the left) go straight across on to a gravel path.

Left: Easy woodland trail through Clumber Park.

Inset: Ornamental gates at the entrance to South Lodge.

4. At the T-junction with the next road turn left, follow it round to the right and cross a ford. Go past a farm on the left and then turn right on to a track opposite red-brick houses.

5. Carefully follow red bike trail signs along the field and through the woods, climbing then descending. At the crossroads with Limetree Avenue go straight ahead.

6. At the junction with the next road (Manton Lodge is to your right) turn left then after $1/4$ mile turn right on to a broad gravel track. Go past a caravan site on the left. At a crossroads of tracks at the top of a gentle climb turn left.

7. At the bottom of the descent at the crossroads just before the barrier and barbecue site turn right. Follow red bike trail signs very carefully through this wooded section.

8. At the road (Clumber Lane) turn right then just after the pay point entry box turn left on to a gravel track.

9. Long gentle descent. At the road turn left then right towards a second pay point entry box. Continue in the same direction to return to the Cycle Hire Centre.

ROUTE 16
CLUMBER PARK (WORKSOP)

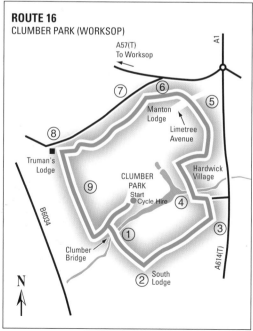

SOUTHWELL TO BILSTHORPE RAILWAY PATH

(12 miles northeast of Nottingham)

You are in Robin Hood Country here with Sherwood Forest just a few miles to the west. It would seem to stretch belief that Robin Hood had much to do with the course of the dismantled railway used in this ride but nevertheless the map shows the Robin Hood Way following the railway path between Southwell and Farnsfield. Although the ride starts from the northern edge of Southwell, it is well worth exploring the centre of this fine old town, especially its magnificent minster. The ride itself is a very pleasant outing through wooded cuttings and rich arable country glimpsed between the hedgerows. Bilsthorpe lies on the eastern edges of what was the great Nottinghamshire coal mining area, almost all of which has disappeared in the last 20 years.

BACKGROUND AND PLACES OF INTEREST

Southwell Minster

The lovely cream-coloured Southwell Minster with its slender towers and spires dates from 1108. There is a magnificent series of stone carvings called 'The Leaves of Southwell' leading to and in the chapter house. Charles I gave himself up to the Scots Commissioners in the nearby 17th-century Saracens Head in 1646.

Below: Once you've found the start of the trail you can't get lost!

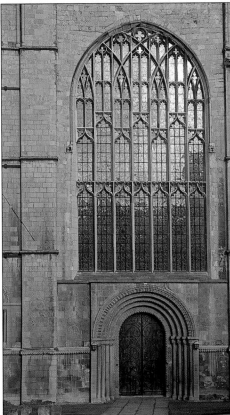

Right: Southwell Minster.

Above: Traffic-free trails give parents peace of mind.

Above Left: Railway path verges are excellent wildlife habitats.

Starting Points and Parking:

1. (Southwell) The car park next to the Newcastle Arms PH, Southwell. From the mini-roundabout by the Saracens Head PH in the centre of Southwell, leave the A612 and follow Queen Street. At the crossroads go straight ahead on to Station Road. Immediately after the Newcastle Arms PH turn left into the car park.

2. (Bilsthorpe) The end of Forest Walk (a new housing estate), signposted 'Picnic Site' at the southern end of Bilsthorpe. Proceeding south from Bilsthorpe along the Kirklington Road, turn off the roundabout on to Forest Walk (opposite the turning to the landfill site).

Distance: 7 miles one way, 14 miles return.

Map: Ordnance Survey Landranger Sheet 120.

Hills: There are no hills.

Surface: Good quality gravel tracks.

Roads and Road Crossings: Several crossings of minor roads.

Refreshments: The Newcastle Arms PH at the start of the trail in Southwell; lots of choice in Southwell itself.

ROUTE INSTRUCTIONS:
The route is well signposted and no instructions are necessary. It runs for 7 miles between Southwell and Bilsthorpe, crossing several minor roads.

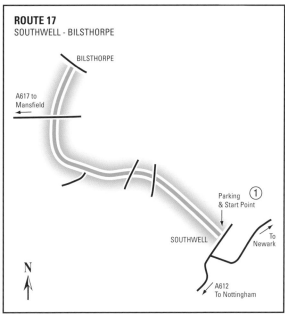

ROUTE 17
SOUTHWELL - BILSTHORPE

BILSTHORPE

A617 to Mansfield

Parking ①
& Start Point

SOUTHWELL

To Newark

A612
To Nottingham

N

A CIRCUIT OF CARSINGTON WATER

(5 miles northeast of Ashbourne)

One of the country's most recently built reservoirs, Carsington Water has quickly established itself as a major focus for recreational cycling, offering a circuit around the lake which is demanding enough to give young children a real sense of achievement when they complete the ride. There are two crossings of the B5035 and about 1 mile is spent on a minor road, but as the latter runs parallel with the main road, very few vehicles have any reason to use it. This lane detours to the lovely stone-built village of Hopton, enabling you to enjoy a stopping point at the pub about three-quarters of the way around the circuit.

BACKGROUND AND PLACES OF INTEREST

Carsington Water

Although planning for the reservoir started in the 1960s, the final go-ahead was not given until 1979. Work was at an advanced stage when part of the original dam collapsed in 1984. The dam was then levelled to its foundations and work on a new design was started in February 1989. Construction was finished in 1991 and the reservoir and Visitor Centre were opened by the Queen in 1992. Most of the water in the reservoir is pumped from the River Derwent when the river level is high. The reservoir is the ninth largest in England — at its highest level it can hold 7,800 million gallons.

Below: Looking across Carsington Water.

Starting Point and Parking: Pay and Display car park at the Visitor Centre at Carsington Water, just off the B5035 to the northwest of Ashbourne.

Distance: 7-mile circuit.

Map/leaflet: Ordnance Survey Landranger Sheet 119. Better is the free map available from the Visitor Centre (01629 540696).

Hills: There are several short, steep hills on the far side of the lake from the Visitor Centre.

Surface: Good quality gravel tracks.

Roads and Road Crossings: Care should be taken on the two crossings of the B5035. There is a 1-mile section on minor lanes through Hopton.

Refreshments: Café at the Visitor Centre; Miners Arms PH in Hopton on the far side of the lake.

Cycle Hire: At the Visitor Centre. (01629 540478).

Right: Unusual sign on the circuit of the lake.

Below: An excellent day out for the family.

ROUTE INSTRUCTIONS:
The route is well signposted.
1. With your back to the Visitor Centre entrance turn left then at the corner of the building continue straight ahead on the broad gravel track.

2. Follow this obvious track with the water to your left, crossing the dam wall, following the frequent signposts.

3. The route becomes hillier! At the main road (B5035) take care crossing on to the minor lane opposite. Follow the waymarks through the village of Hopton, past the Miners Arms PH.

4. At the second crossing of the B5035 take care as you go straight ahead towards the car park then bear right at the fork and follow this track for 2 miles back to the start.

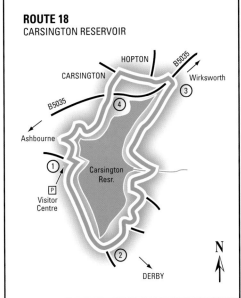

ROUTE 18
CARSINGTON RESERVOIR

🚲 ROUTE 19

THE NUTBROOK TRAIL FROM SHIPLEY COUNTRY PARK TO LONG EATON
(West of Nottingham)

Shipley Country Park has many fine tracks within its 600 acres of landscaped parkland — should you not feel up to a 16-mile there-and-back ride to Long Eaton there are plenty of shorter options within the park itself. There are also the temptations of the American Theme Park which is situated right next door. Once you have negotiated your way up and down the hill and past the Theme Park you find yourself on a railway path that runs along the course of the old Stanton branch line for

Below: The Erewash Canal towpath.

Right: A green corridor through Sandiacre.

5 miles down to the Erewash Canal, linking Eastwood with the River Trent at Trentlock, south of Long Eaton. You pass many fine red-brick buildings along the banks of the canal before the trail drops you somewhat abruptly in the middle of Long Eaton.

BACKGROUND AND PLACES OF INTEREST

Shipley Country Park
Located on the edge of Heanor and Ilkeston, less than 10 miles from Derby, Shipley Country Park offers 600 acres of attractive varied landscape and 1,000 years of history. Shipley was developed in the 18th century as a country estate and coal mining area by the influential Miller-Mundy family. Following the demise of the old coal mines and opencast quarries, former railways have been transformed into leafy pathways, old reservoirs are now tranquil lakes teeming with wildlife and reclaimed spoil heaps are now large woodlands, rolling hills and wildflower meadows. The park was opened in 1976.

Stanton Lock

Starting Points and Parking: 1. Shipley Country Park, off the A608/A6007 to the west of Nottingham (Grid Reference 431452). 2. Long Eaton (southwest of Nottingham), by Asda and the Council Offices. Turn off the roundabout on the A6005 in the centre of Long Eaton signposted 'Superstore, Town Hall, Sandiacre Cycle Route'.

Distance: 8 miles one way, 16 miles return.

Map: Ordnance Survey Landranger Sheet 129.

Hills: There is one hill.

Surface: Good quality gravel tracks.

Roads and Road Crossings: None.

Refreshments: At Shipley Country Park; lots of choice in Long Eaton.

Cycle Hire: At Shipley Country Park (01773 719961).

ROUTE INSTRUCTIONS:
The route is well signposted.
1. From the Information Board in the car park in Shipley Country Park take the gravel track signposted 'Public bridleway, Osborne Pond'. At a crossroads of tracks go straight ahead to join the railway path through the wood.

2. The track turns to tarmac. At the crossroads with the lane (with Coppice House Business Centre to your right) turn right and go downhill. Continue in the same direction, staying on the tarmac path, at one point jinking left then right. Climb then descend alongside the Theme Park.

3. At the T-junction at the end of the Theme Park turn right then shortly take the first tarmac track to the left opposite a red-brick house. Follow the tarmac path for 5 miles.

4. At the canal turn right (remember this point for the return route).

Left: A series of locks near to Long Eaton.

Right: Taking a break at Ilkeston Lakes.

5. Easy to miss! After 3 miles, just after passing the back of Andy Supermarket to your right, by a lock and a hump-back red-brick bridge, turn left by a Nutbrook Trail signpost on to a path running parallel with the towpath.

6. Follow the trail as it swings left past a tall red-brick chimney, passing through a barrier then turning right on to a tarmac path. The trail ends near Asda and the Town Hall in the centre of Long Eaton.

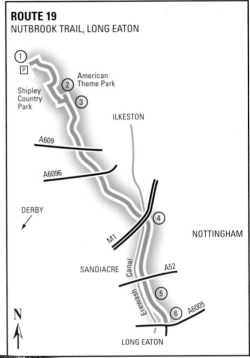

ROUTE 19
NUTBROOK TRAIL, LONG EATON

🚲 ROUTE 20

DERBY TO WORTHINGTON RAILWAY PATH

This route out of Derby was one of the first built by Sustrans, the Bristol-based engineering charity which was awarded £43 million in 1995 by the National Lottery to build Britain's National Cycle Network. The route has many of the best features of a Sustrans project — it starts from the very heart of the city and uses an attractive riverside path, canal towpath and a disused railway on its way from the urban centre into the heart of the countryside. Schools and colleges benefit from safe cycling routes for schoolchildren and students whilst recreational cyclists and those with young children living in Derby near the route do not have to worry about driving to the start of a cycle route as it is right there on their doorstep! As the route moves out into the countryside you will come across some beautifully painted Millennium Mileposts and some very fine stone sculptures. The ride ends at Worthington which has a curious red-brick octagonal lock-up and a pub at the far end of the village.

This Page: Derby city centre.

Above: The path alongside the River Derwent.

BACKGROUND AND PLACES OF INTEREST

Swarkestone
The village lies half a mile from the Trent & Mersey Canal, beside the River Trent. Its bridge and causeway date back to the 13th century and are reputed to be the most southerly point Bonnie Prince Charlie reached on his march to London.

Breedon on the Hill
On a limestone bluff above the village stands the Norman church of St Mary and St Hardulph with its magnificent 8th-century Saxon frieze, Iron Age hillfort and views of the Trent valley.

Starting Points and Parking: 1. Riverside Gardens in the centre of Derby (near the bus station and the Eagle Centre Market). 2. If coming from outside Derby it is best to start (and park) at the south end of the trail in Worthington. From the crossroads in Worthington by St Matthew's Church follow Breedon Lane downhill, signposted 'Cloud Trail', then shortly turn first right and follow this to the car park.

Distance: 13 miles one way, 26 miles return.

Maps: Ordnance Survey Landranger Sheets 128 and 129.

Hills: There are no hills.

Surface: Good quality gravel tracks.

Roads and Road Crossings: Two busy roads in Derby are crossed safely via toucan crossings. There is a short road section if you wish to go for refreshments in Worthington.

Refreshments: Lots of choice in Derby; Swarkestone Tearooms, at the Lock House at the start of the canal section; lots of choice in Melbourne (1 mile off the route); the Malt Shovel PH, Worthington (³/₄ mile on quiet roads beyond the end of the trail).

ROUTE INSTRUCTIONS:
1. The ride starts in the Riverside Gardens in the centre of Derby (near the bus station and the council offices). Follow signs for the Riverside Path and stay close to the river for 2 miles.

2. Go past Pride Park (the stadium for Derby County Football Club), pass beneath a low black bridge (with attached pipe!) then take the second of two closely spaced paths to the right.

3. Go past a lake then take the next right past the college buildings. Keep bearing left to pass beneath a bridge. After 1 mile, cross three roads in quick succession, the first and the third using toucan crossings.

4. After a further mile, near the end of the built-up area, at a crossroads with a minor lane go straight ahead, signposted 'Swarkestone Lock'. ('Sinfin' is signposted to the right.)

5. Pass beneath the A50, cross a bridge over the canal then turn left on to the towpath signposted 'Melbourne'.

6. After 2 miles, just before the large bridge over the river bear right and join the railway path.

7. After 4 miles the path veers right and runs parallel with the A42. Cross the bridge over the dual carriageway then bear left to rejoin the railway path.

8. After 1¹/₂ miles the trail ends. If you wish to visit Worthington with its attractive church, octagonal lock-up and pub, turn left on to the minor lane then at the crossroads at the end of Breedon Lane turn left on to Church Street, signposted 'Griffydam, Osgathorpe'. Follow this road through the village for ³/₄ mile past the octagonal red-brick lock-up to the Malt Shovel pub.

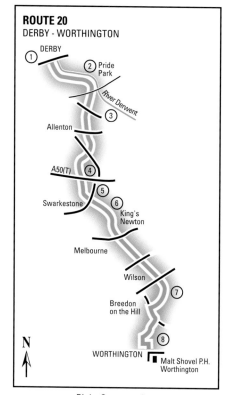

ROUTE 20
DERBY - WORTHINGTON

DERBY
①
② Pride Park
River Derwent
③
Allenton
A50(T) ④
⑤
Swarkestone ⑥
King's Newton
Melbourne
Wilson
⑦
Breedon on the Hill
⑧
WORTHINGTON ■ Malt Shovel P.H. Worthington

N

Right: Stone sculptures on the path near Worthington.

The octagonal lock-up in Worthington.

ON TOP OF THE LONG MYND NEAR CHURCH STRETTON

This is not a recognised cycle trail in the same way as a railway path or a waymarked forestry route is, it is merely a suggested route along a bridleway on top of a spectacular range of hills with the most magnificent views on a clear day. As such, it is not worth doing in poor visibility as the whole point of the ride is the views! It is one of the few rides in the country where you should beware of gliders that are taking off or landing — the route passes right by a gliding club that is set high on the Long Mynd for obvious reasons — better chance of take-off and superb views once aloft. It is suggested that you turn around a couple of miles beyond the Gliding Club where the gradient of the bridleway suddenly steepens but if you are feeling very brave and very fit there is nothing to stop you devising a circular ride on a mixture of quiet lanes and bridleways, dropping steeply down into the valley of the River Onny then climbing back up to the starting point at Shooting Box.

Right: There is a splendid ridge ride along the Long Mynd.

NB This is one of the toughest rides in the book and should only be attempted on mountain bikes. It is not suitable for very young children and involves a long steady climb of almost 400ft back to the starting point. That said, it is an exhilarating ride with fantastic views on a clear day.

BACKGROUND AND PLACES OF INTEREST

Church Stretton
The half-timbered houses date from the town's late 19th-century boom as a health resort.

Starting Point and Parking: The Long Mynd is just off the A49 above Church Stretton. From the centre of Church Stretton follow signs for 'Burway/Long Mynd'. Follow this very steep and narrow road to the top of the hill. At the fork at the top bear right signposted 'Youth Hostel'. Just before the start of the descent there is a small, grassy car park to the right by a wooden post with 'Shooting Box' on it.

Distance: 5 miles one way, 10 miles return.

Map: Ordnance Survey Landranger Sheet 137.

Hills: Despite following the ridge this ride has several hills, most notably on the return to the car park from the Gliding Club (almost 400ft of climbing).

Surface: A mixture of good stone tracks and grassy tracks with the occasional rough section. Mountain bikes are highly recommended.

Roads and Road Crossings: Care should be taken on the short section along the public road near the Gliding Club.

Refreshments: None on the route, plenty of choice in Church Stretton.

ROUTE INSTRUCTIONS:
1. From the Shooting Box car park cross the road on to the climbing track opposite, signposted 'Polebank'. Continue climbing, going straight ahead at a crossroads of tracks to reach the summit and the toposcope showing all the surrounding hills.

2. Descend to the road, bear right and continue descending. Climb then descend again. At the Midland Gliding Club bear left on the road and pass to the left of the club building (beware of gliders!).

3. At the major fork of tracks with a 'No Right of Way' sign to the left, bear right on the lower, grassy track signposted 'Plowden'.

4. It is suggested that you continue for a further 2 miles until the land starts dropping away steeply. Retrace your route, taking care on the lane section.

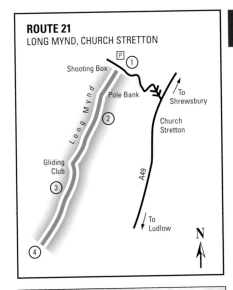

ROUTE 21
LONG MYND, CHURCH STRETTON

Above: Big views from the end of the Long Mynd ridge.

Left: Beware of gliders as you go past the flying club.

THE SILKIN WAY, SOUTH OF TELFORD

This ride is in the heart of the area where the Industrial Revolution started: the iron bridge over the River Severn at (unsurprisingly!) the village of Ironbridge was a major step on the route which saw Great Britain rise to industrial pre-eminence throughout the world in the late 18th century and most of the 19th century. The iron wheel used as the motif for the Silkin Way is an indication of the area's industrial past. The route starts in the heart of the New Town of Telford and uses a dismantled railway for much of its course, passing through deep rock cuttings and thickly wooded stretches. The Severn is reached at Coalport where there is a pub on the other side of the lovely bridge over the river.

BACKGROUND AND PLACES OF INTEREST

The Birthplace of the Industrial Revolution
At Coalbrookdale in 1709, Abraham Darby started to experiment with methods of smelting iron ore using coke instead of charcoal. From his modest beginnings as a maker of iron-bellied pots and household pans, Darby's clever innovations were later used to create monsters! Two of these iron monsters, David and Sampson, now feature in the Open Air Museum at Blists Hill. They are two mighty furnace engines that together gave sterling service for just over a century, pumping air into the Priorslee furnace, like a giant pair of bellows.

Below: The ornate bridge over the River Severn at Coalport.

ROUTE 22
SILKIN WAY, TELFORD

TELFORD
M54
① ← Start & parking in Town Park
② Town Park
A442
③
A4169
④
■ Museum
Blists Hill
River Severn
Coalport
⑤
N ↑
Woodbridge Inn
IRONBRIDGE

Starting Point and Parking: The car park for Town Park in the centre of Telford (1 mile southeast of M54 Jct 5).

Distance: 5 miles one way, 10 miles return.

Map: Ordnance Survey Landranger Sheet 127.

Hills: There are no hills.

Surface: Tarmac or good quality gravel tracks.

Roads and Road Crossings: Several crossings of minor roads.

Refreshments: Lots of choice in Telford; Woodbridge Inn at Coalport.

ROUTE INSTRUCTIONS:
The route is signposted with an iron wheel logo.
1. From the Town Park car park in the centre of Telford go into the park through the green metal gates, continue straight ahead along a road with humps and a white painted cycle lane (pass to the right of the public conveniences).

2. Exit the park, ignore two car parks to the left and take the next left downhill by a black metal barrier and a wooden 'Silkin Way' signpost. Descend to cross the bridge and turn sharp right. Continue in the same direction along the railway path, taking good care to remember this point for the return trip, as it is very easy to miss heading in the opposite direction!

3. Pass beneath four bridges, cross Chapel Lane on to a continuation of the railway path. Cross a second minor lane. Shortly, pass beneath the road bridge and turn right (there is a wooden 'Silkin Way' signpost). This soon runs on the pavement alongside the main road, passing the turn to Blists Hill Victorian Town.

Above Right: A lime kiln along the trail.

Bottom Right: The China Museum at Coalport.

4. Go beneath two narrow metal bridges and follow the pavement as it bears left away from the road.

5. At the T-junction by the Brewery Inn go straight ahead on to a continuation of the path then bear right to arrive at the end of the path, Coalport Bridge and the Woodbridge Inn.

CANNOCK CHASE, NORTH OF BIRMINGHAM
(5 miles southeast of Stafford)

Together with the woodland around Sherwood Forest, Cannock Chase is the largest Forestry Commission holding in the area covered by this book. In character it is far from the dense blocks of conifers that cloak hillsides in Wales and Scotland — there are many open, sandy spaces, a pleasant mixture of broadleaf and coniferous trees and, more important from the cyclist's point of view, a large network of bridleways, many of which are well-drained broad stone-based tracks where it is possible to cycle all year round. The ride described is a waymarked route through the forest — waymarkings are always a blessing because it is notoriously difficult to give adequate route directions to guide people through a forest where the only noticeable features are trees, tracks and hills! The ride is largely a descent in the first half along the course of Sherbrook Valley and largely a climb in the second half up Abraham's Valley.

BACKGROUND AND PLACES OF INTEREST

Cannock Chase
The remnant of a vast royal hunting forest (chase). At 17,000 acres it is the smallest mainland Area of Outstanding Natural Beauty in Britain. Much of Cannock Chase is recognised by English Nature as a Site of Special Scientific Interest.

Main Picture: Broad forest tracks through Cannock Chase.

Inset: Clearings in the forest offer fine views.

Starting Point and Parking: At the Cannock Chase Visitor Centre, 4 miles southwest of Rugeley (Grid Reference 005154). Turn off the A460 on to the B5013 towards Cannock then first right on to the minor road (Brindley Heath Road). The Visitor Centre is about 1 mile along this road, on the right.

Distance: 9-mile circuit.

Maps/leaflet: Ordnance Survey Landranger Sheets 127 and 128. More useful is the map called *Discover Cannock Chase* that you can buy for 25p from the Visitor Centre.

Hills: There are several hills. The ride is mainly downhill in the first half and uphill in the second!

Surface: A mixture of good quality gravel tracks with some rougher sections. Mountain bikes are recommended.

Roads and Road Crossings: Care should be taken crossing the two roads on the circuit. There is a short section on a minor road.

Refreshments: None on the route. There is a pub in Little Haywood, just to the north of the lowest point of the ride (at the bottom of Sherbrook Valley, near Route Instruction 6). Otherwise you will need to go into Cannock or Rugeley.

ROUTE INSTRUCTIONS:
The route is well signposted.
1. Exit the Visitor Centre car park back towards the road. Turn right, following the green and white bike signs, passing the overflow car park to your right. At the T-junction by the tall pines turn left.

2. At the T-junction at the end of Marquis Drive turn right (take care). Just before the crossroads and the 'Give Way' sign cross the road on to the cyclepath and continue straight ahead at the next road on to a woodland track.

3. Keep following the green bike signs. You will need to turn right then left at

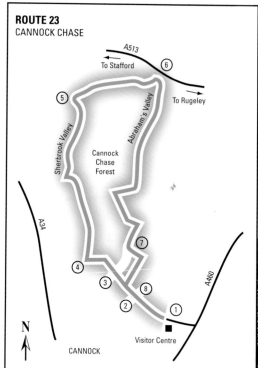

ROUTE 23
CANNOCK CHASE

two T-junctions. At the road continue straight ahead.

4. At the T-junction at the bottom of the descent turn left. At the bottom of the dip, just before the path starts climbing again turn right to continue downhill.

5. Continue in the same direction, basically downhill although there is one short climb on a sweeping bend. At the crossroads at the bottom of a long descent, by a 'Stepping Stones' signpost turn right.

6. At the T-junction (with a car park away to your left) turn right uphill. Steep then steady climb.

7. Go past a low red-brick building (Army Cadet Force). At the crossroads with the road go straight ahead on to a narrow track (take care crossing the road). At the T-junction with the wide forest track turn right then right again. After a few hundred yards turn left to rejoin the outward route.

8. Cross the road then bear left on to the next road for 100yds. Take the first road to the left (Marquis Drive) then first right to return to the Visitor Centre.

Below: Dappled woodland sunlight.

Inset: The route is well-waymarked throughout.

🚲 ROUTE 24

ASHBY WOULDS
HERITAGE TRAIL
(9 miles southeast of Burton upon Trent)

The signboards along this short railway path ride to the northeast of Measham offer a clear explanation not only of the area's industrial history but also of the huge efforts needed to restore nature's balance after more than 150 years of dumping mining and industrial waste without thinking of the long-term environmental consequences. As a result of these huge efforts, lakes, grassland and woodland have been created where before there were stagnant hazardous pools and a moonscape of spoils. Within a generation the area will be covered by mature trees and a visitor would never know what had previously been there! In addition to the 7-mile there-and-back ride along the railway path there are three different circuits of between 1 and 2 miles in what is now called Donisthorpe Woodland.

This Spread: Donisthorpe Woodlands.

Ashby & Nuneaton Joint Railway

Opened in 1873, the railway was built to transport coal from the local pits to London and the Southeast. The line closed to regular passenger traffic in 1931 and the last goods train ran in 1981.

Bath Pit

This pit was sunk in 1806 and closed in 1854. Whilst sinking the shaft the miners hit a saline spring at a depth of 600ft. This became the source of Moira Spa. However, many people were put off by the proximity to the colliery so a new Bath House was built at Ashby de la Zouch. It was completed in 1826 and thrived for many years using Moira water.

Moira Furnace

Opened in 1806 to extract iron ore from the coal deposits already being mined in the Ashby Woulds area, it only remained operational for 11 months due to the variability in quantity and quality of the product.

Measham

The town developed around mining interests in the 19th and 20th centuries and became one of the main centres of the Industrial Revolution largely as a result of the efforts of Joseph Wilkes who bought the manor in 1777. He was a banker, a coalmine owner, a brick producer and mill owner. He introduced the first steam engine in the area for his mill.

Below: Wild flowers tumble from the verges.

Starting Point and Parking: The ride starts from the car park by the library in the centre of the village of Measham, just off the M42/A42 to the northeast of Junction 11 (9 miles southeast of Burton upon Trent).

Distance: 3¹/₂ miles one way, 7 miles return. There are also rides in the newly created Donisthorpe Woodland Park:
Green route — Woodland Park Circular — 2.4 km;
Purple route — Hill Street Circular — 1.8 km;
Orange route — Moira Road Circular — 1.6km.

Inset: No chance of getting lost on the Heritage Trail.

Map: Ordnance Survey Landranger Sheet 128.

Hills: There are no hills.

Surface: Good quality gravel tracks.

Roads and Road Crossings: None.

Refreshments: Lots of choice in Measham; the Navigation Inn on the B5004 to the northeast of Overseal, at the end of the trail.

ROUTE INSTRUCTIONS:
The route is well signposted.
1. From the car park by the library in the centre of Measham follow the 'Ashby Woulds Heritage Trail' signposts.

2. After ³/₄ mile turn left to join the pavement alongside the road that passes beneath the A42, then shortly, at the next Heritage Trail signpost, turn right to rejoin the railway path.

3. Follow the blue arrows through Donisthorpe Woodland (the other coloured waymarks refer to circular rides within the park).

4. The trail ends at the Navigation Inn on the B5004 (northeast of Overseal).

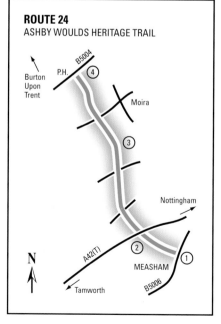

ROUTE 24
ASHBY WOULDS HERITAGE TRAIL

🚲 ROUTE 25

CANALS THROUGH BIRMINGHAM

Although it is often stated that Birmingham has more miles of canals than Venice, (there are over 130 miles of canals in Birmingham and the Black Country) this does not translate, unfortunately, into a fine network of broad, smooth, gravel towpaths that would immeasurably improve the life of every cyclist in Birmingham. With the exception of the Main Line Canal between Birmingham and Wolverhampton, cycling is undertaken on a de facto rather than a de jure basis. The Wolverhampton & Birmingham Canal has been included because the surface is excellent, the towpath broad, the cyclists numerous and it is used for a short section by Sustrans' National Cycle Network. The route to the south ends abruptly at King's Norton Tunnel, one of the longest in the country. The hub of the canal network in Birmingham lies around Digbeth Basin and Gas Street Basin. To the northwest the canal from Birmingham to Wolverhampton, known simply as the Birmingham Canal or the Main Line, is variable in quality and rarely pretty — this is a trip past the sinews of a muscular, industrial city with metal foundries and hot metal smells. As the Birmingham Canal in its entirety forms part of the National Cycle Network it may be assumed that over the next five years it will all be improved to the excellent standard to be enjoyed near the centre of the city.

BACKGROUND AND PLACES OF INTEREST

The Main Line Canal from Birmingham to Wolverhampton

By 1769, the engineer James Brindley had completed the first of Birmingham's canals from Wednesbury to Newhall then to a wharf, beyond Gas Street Basin, where the Holiday Inn now stands. By 1772 the Old Main Line extended to Wolverhampton. The canal created rapid growth in industry — coal and building supplies were brought in and manufactured goods carried out. In the next half century the canal system spread rapidly and expanding trade brought great congestion. In the 1820s Thomas Telford constructed a straight canal, the New Main Line, running parallel at a lower level to the Old Main Line. Despite advances in canal planning, the Galton Valley cutting was still dug out by men using picks, shovels and wheelbarrows.

Below: The new heart of Birmingham.

Starting Point and Parking: The National Indoor Arena in the centre of Birmingham.

Distance: (a) Birmingham to Wolverhampton — 14 miles one way, 28 miles return. (b) Birmingham to King's Norton Tunnel — 6 miles one way, 12 miles return.

Left: The church at King's Norton.

Below: Superb towpath alongside the Worcester & Birmingham Canal.

Map/leaflet: Ordnance Survey Landranger Sheet 139. A street map of Birmingham is more useful.

Hills: There are no hills.

Surface: The Worcester & Birmingham towpath is a good quality gravel track. The first section of the Birmingham to Wolverhampton Canal is very good but there are also some rough sections.

Roads and Road Crossings: None.

Refreshments: Cafés and pubs in the centre of the city.

ROUTE INSTRUCTIONS:
1. From the centre of Birmingham to Wolverhampton.
With your back to the National Indoor Arena turn right, with the water to your left. There are occasionally paths on both sides of the canal. Keep an eye out for the signs indicating where you change sides. The path can be followed for up to 14 miles to Wolverhampton. You may wish to turn around when the surface deteriorates.

2. From the centre of Birmingham along the Worcester & Birmingham Canal to King's Norton Tunnel.
Start from the Gas Street Basin in the centre of Birmingham. Follow signs for the Worcester & Birmingham Canal for 6 miles as far as King's Norton Tunnel.

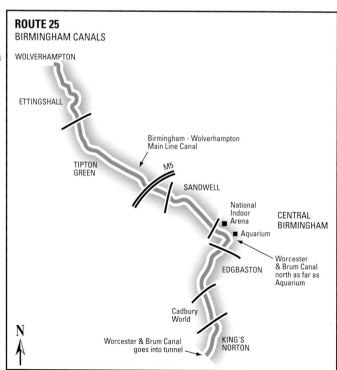

ROUTE 25
BIRMINGHAM CANALS

WOLVERHAMPTON

ETTINGSHALL

Birmingham - Wolverhampton Main Line Canal

TIPTON GREEN

M5

SANDWELL

National Indoor Arena

CENTRAL BIRMINGHAM

Aquarium

Worcester & Brum Canal north as far as Aquarium

EDGBASTON

Cadbury World

Worcester & Brum Canal goes into tunnel

KING'S NORTON

N

ROUTE 26

SUTTON PARK, NORTH OF BIRMINGHAM
(North Birmingham)

Sutton Park is one of those parks on the edge of a large city (not unlike Richmond Park in London) where you often have to remind yourself that you are less than a couple of miles from a huge conurbation where millions of people are living and working. Sutton Park offers a sense of wide open spaces, with grassland and woodland and a plethora of tracks to explore. The park has considerably improved since through traffic was banned some two years ago. There is no specifically waymarked cycle trail — this route is just one of many that you could easily devise yourself. The best way to appreciate the park fully is by buying the map from the Visitor Centre and giving yourself plenty of time to explore — the map will tell you the areas where cycling is **not** allowed.

Far Right: Tracks and car-free roads criss-cross Sutton Park.

Below: Sutton Park is Birmingham's green lung.

Inset: Gorse bush in flower alongside the trail.

Starting Point and Parking: The car park by the Visitor Centre just to the west of the A5127 in Sutton Coldfield.

Distance: 3-mile circuit.

Map/leaflet: Ordnance Survey Landranger Sheet 139. Much more useful is the map of Sutton Park that can be purchased from the Visitor Centre.

Hills: Gently undulating.

Surface: Good quality gravel tracks.

Roads and Road Crossings: The roads are all barred to through traffic.

Refreshments: Café in the park.

ROUTE INSTRUCTIONS:
1. From the Visitor Centre climb up to the four-way junction of roads ('Keepers Pool Only' is signposted straight ahead). Do not go towards Keepers Pool but turn left on the road with a single gate barrier.

2. At a major junction of tracks go straight ahead. At a tarmac crossroads just beyond a barrier turn right, passing a car parking area on your left. Go through the next barrier.

3. At the Jamboree Stone turn left on to a broad, red gravel track.

4. Fast descent. Cross the stream. Easy to miss! 200yds before the main road (you will hear the traffic and glimpse it through the trees) turn left on to a less well-defined path. There is a signpost down to your left: 'Ground nesting birds — please keep dogs on lead'.

5. Continue straight ahead on the main track through the woodland. Go through the car park and turn left on to the road. Go past Longmoor Pool.

6. At a tarmac crossroads go straight ahead through a wooden barrier to rejoin the outward route back to the Visitor Centre.

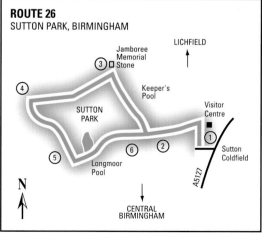

REA VALLEY ROUTE, SOUTH OF BIRMINGHAM

Forming part of the National Cycle Network through Birmingham, the Rea Valley Route follows the River Rea (at times more like a stream!) through the delights of Cannon Hill Park where there are always fantastic displays of flowers, shrubs and rare and ornamental trees. Beyond Cannon Hill Park the ride follows a tarmac path alongside the river through Stirchley and on to a short section of the Worcester & Birmingham Canal, explored more fully in Ride 25 'Canals through Birmingham'. It ends at King's Norton Park where there is a playground for children. Beyond this point there are plans for the National Route to continue alongside the river to Longbridge then turn west to Waseley Hills Country Park. To the north of Cannon Hill Park the National Route will use traffic-calmed streets and specially-built cyclists' contraflow lanes to take you right into Centenary Square.

BACKGROUND AND PLACES OF INTEREST

The River Rea

Fifteen miles long and rising southwest of Birmingham in Waseley Country Park, the River Rea flows northeast across the city to join the River Tame near Spaghetti Junction. Although a small river, it has been called the 'Mother of Birmingham' as it has played a vital role in the development of the city, particularly in the Digbeth area where there was a small settlement hundreds of years ago. Over 20 mills once flourished along the Rea Valley, many of them built for corn grinding but during the Industrial Revolution they provided water power for Birmingham's industries.

This Spread: The Rea Valley Route offers a lovely escape from the city.

Starting Points and Parking: 1. Cannon Hill Park, central Birmingham. The car park lies off the A441 (Pershore Road), just to the south of Edgbaston Cricket Ground. 2. King's Norton Park, on Westhill Road, just south of the junction of the A441 Pershore Road with the A4040 Watford Road and B4121 Middleton Road.

Distance: 4 miles one way, 8 miles return.

Map: Ordnance Survey Landranger Sheet 139.

Hills: None.

Surface: Tarmac or good quality gravel tracks.

Roads and Road Crossings: All busy roads are crossed at toucan crossings.

Refreshments: Café in Cannon Hill Park.

ROUTE INSTRUCTIONS:
The route is well signposted.
1. From the lodge at the north end of Cannon Hill Park follow the cycle track through the park. Continue in the same direction with the river close by to your right.

2. The tarmac path swings right to cross the river via a brick and metal bridge. Shortly, the track joins Kitchener Road. Turn first left on to Cecil Road then at the T-junction turn left then right on to a continuation of the riverside path.

3. Follow the Rea Valley Route and signs for 'Stirchley, King's Norton'. At the next busy road (Cartland Road) go straight ahead via a toucan crossing on to a continuation of the riverside path.

4. At the T-junction with the trading estate road turn right to cross the bridge, then immediately left. At the crossroads with busy Fordhouse Lane use the toucan crossing to go straight ahead, signposted 'King's Norton, Northfield'.

5. At the end of the cyclepath by a tall wooden signpost turn left on the quiet estate road (Dacer Close) then shortly first left. Follow Rea Valley Route signs to join the Worcester

& Birmingham Canal towpath. Turn left along the towpath.

6. At the second bridge over the canal you will need to cross to the towpath on the other side. Easy to miss. Immediately after passing a red-brick bridge (with a '72' plaque on it) turn right by a large red-brick house away from the towpath signposted 'Rea Valley Route. King's Norton'. Cross the playing fields then cross Pershore Road. The ride ends at the west edge of King's Norton Park (at the junction of Wychall Lane and Westhill Road).

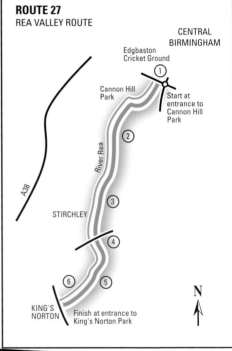

ROUTE 27
REA VALLEY ROUTE

Inset: Tea rooms in Cannon Hill Park.

Magnificent ornamental trees in Cannon Hill Park.

Inset: Sustrans Millennium Milepost for the National Cycle Network.

THE MARKET HARBOROUGH ARM OF THE GRAND UNION CANAL

Britain has 2,000 miles of canals but only a small fraction of the towpaths are suitable for recreational cycling — the majority are too narrow, too rough, too muddy, too overgrown or a combination of all four. The Market Harborough Arm of the Grand Union Canal is a splendid exception and offers a fine 12-mile there-and-back ride with good views, refreshments at a pub known as Bridge 61 and a chance to visit the museum at Foxton Locks. The winding course of the canal is explained by the desire of the canal builders to hug the contours and thus avoid the need to build any locks. As the height they followed is at about 300ft there are some fine views out into the surrounding countryside. The banks are crowded with wild flowers and hawthorn blossom in the late spring and early summer; cow parsley, campion, vetch and willow-herb add shades of white, pink and purple. There are myriad bridges with names that must all tell stories — Uncle Tom's Bridge, Rainbow Bridge, Pats Bridge and Black Horse Bridge amongst others. It is suggested you turn around at Debdale Wharf Bridge; at this point the towpath turns to grass and the going becomes a lot rougher.

BACKGROUND AND PLACES OF INTEREST

Market Harborough

Next to the town's handsome ironstone church is a fine timber-framed building built in 1614 as a butter market 'to keepe the market people drye in time of fowle weather'. It was then used as a grammar school until 1892.

Foxton Locks

The 10 locks at Foxton opened in 1814. They raise the canal by 75ft and take an average of 45 minutes to negotiate, using 25,000 gallons of water per passage. The locks linked the Leicestershire & Northamptonshire Union Canal and the (Old) Grand Union Canal. Following a takeover by the Grand Junction Canal, a lift was opened in 1900 to compete against the railways for traffic. It was part of a scheme to widen the route from the Derbyshire coalfields to London. The locks were refurbished for night traffic in 1909 but in 1911 the lift was mothballed to save money and the machinery was sold for scrap in 1928.

Below: The old butter market in the centre of Market Harborough.

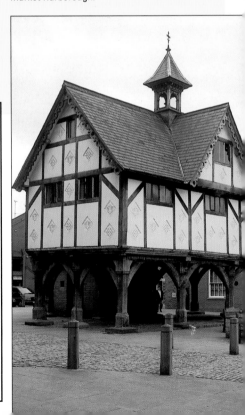

ROUTE 28
GRAND UNION CANAL, MARKET HARBOROUGH

DEBDALE WHARF

Grand Union Canal

FOXTON

Locks

CORBY

MARKET HARBOROUGH

N

A4304

A508

To Northampton

Starting Point and Parking: From the centre of Market Harborough follow signs for 'Melton (Mowbray) B6047' and 'St Lukes Hospital'. After passing a garage then the Police Headquarters turn left (before reaching the roundabout) immediately before the Union Inn Hotel signposted 'Union Wharf South'.

Distance: 6 miles one way, 12 miles return.

Map: Ordnance Survey Landranger Sheet 141.

Hills: There are no hills.

Surface: Good quality gravel track.

Roads and Road Crossings: None.

Refreshments: Café and Bridge 61 PH, Foxton Locks (at the junction with the Grand Union Canal).

ROUTE INSTRUCTIONS:
1. The canal towpath starts near the Union Inn Hotel on the B6047 (Melton Mowbray road). From the hotel follow signs for 'Union Wharf South'.

2. Follow the canal towpath for 6 miles, passing through Foxton. It is suggested that you go as far as Debdale Wharf. After this the towpath becomes grassy and rougher.

Above: The towpath is well-surfaced as far as Debdale Wharf.

Left: Swans and cygnets along the Grand Union Canal.

A CIRCUIT OF PITSFORD WATER IN BRIXWORTH COUNTRY PARK
(6 miles north of Northampton)

This recently completed cycle trail around Pitsford Water is a model of its kind, keeping you close to the water for the whole circuit on well-maintained paths and avoiding time spent on roads, which is so often the failing of circuits around reservoirs. The lake appears to be popular with swans, anglers and windsurfers and if the wind is blowing strongly you may well witness some pretty amazing acrobatics by top-class windsurfers whizzing over the surface of the lake and turning on a sixpence! Nearby is the Brampton Valley Way, a 14-mile railway path between Northampton and Market Harborough, so if you are left with a taste for more cycling after completing the circuit of the lake why not try the railway path as well?

Above: Windsurfers make the most of the strong winds.

BACKGROUND AND PLACES OF INTEREST

Pitsford Water
Anglian Water, in conjunction with Northamptonshire County Council, has been successful in gaining a grant from the Millennium Fund to provide 'Access for All' at Pitsford Water. Brixworth Country Park is being developed to include special gardens and ponds, tracks suitable for disabled access and a link to the Brampton Valley Way. It is intended that the project will provide an opportunity for everyone to experience the wonderful countryside around Pitsford Water.

ROUTE 29
PITSFORD WATER, (BRIXWORTH)

Brixworth

A508

Brixworth Country Park ①

Visitor Centre ■

③

A508 to Northampton

Pitsford

Pitsford Water

② Causeway

Holcot P.H.

N

Above: Fishing boats o shores of the reservoir

Starting Point and Parking: The car park at the Visitor Centre, 6 miles north of Northampton.

Distance: 8-mile circuit of the lake.

Maps/leaflet: Ordnance Survey Landranger Sheets 141 and 152. Much more useful is the map you can get from the cycle hire company.

Hills: There are no hills.

Surface: Good quality gravel tracks.

Roads and Road Crossings: The pavement is used on the road across the causeway.

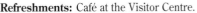

Refreshments: Café at the Visitor Centre.

Cycle Hire: Pitsford Water Cycle Hire (01604 881777).

ROUTE INSTRUCTIONS:
The route is well signposted.
1. From the Visitor Centre, head downhill towards the masts of the dinghies. At the main track around the reservoir turn left, keeping the water to your right.

2. After 2¹/₂ miles, at the T-junction with the road, turn right, cross the causeway across the reservoir, climb gently then turn right through a gate and bear left through the car park (ie once through the gate do not turn immediately right on the earth track).

3. Stay on the gravel track all the way around the reservoir. Cross a second bridge. Ignore the first right into the sailing club. Take the next right then turn left to return to the Visitor Centre.

Left: The broad cycle track around Pitsford Water.

THE RIVER NENE THROUGH PETERBOROUGH

This traffic-free ride on either side of the River Nene from Ferry Meadows Country Park to the centre of Peterborough is part of a much larger and more ambitious project known as the Peterborough Green Wheel. This is a network of cycleways, footpaths and bridleways that will provide safe, continuous routes around the city and 'spokes' linking the Wheel to residential areas and the city centre. The Green Wheel celebrates over 2,000 years of Peterborough's social, cultural, economic and environmental history through a series of sculptures and colourful interpretation boards along the route. Half the cost is met by National Lottery funding through the Millennium Commission and the remainder is raised through sponsorship and donations.

BACKGROUND AND PLACES OF INTEREST

Peterborough
Originally founded around a Saxon monastery, Peterborough has a wealth of history and some outstanding local attractions. The 12th-century cathedral has a unique painted wooden ceiling and is the burial place of Henry VIII's first Queen, Catherine of Aragon. Peterborough Museum & Art Gallery houses some of the finest Jurassic fossils in the country, discovered in the Peterborough area, some of the earliest Christian silverware and exquisite carvings made by Napoleonic prisoners of war.

Main Picture: Riverside development in the centre of Peterborough.

Inset: Peterborough's Green Wheel is a network of traffic-free paths.

Starting Points and Parking: 1. The bridge by Asda in the centre of Peterborough. 2. The Ferry Meadows Country Park (off the Oundle Road, A605).

Distance: 10-mile circuit.

Map/leaflet: Ordnance Survey Landranger Sheet 142. Much better is the leaflet *The Peterborough Millennium Green Wheel — Cycle Map* available from Peterborough Environment City Trust, High Street, Fletton, Peterborough PE2 8DT (Tel: 01733 760883).

Hills: There are no hills.

Surface: Good quality tracks, mainly sealed.

Roads and Road Crossings: No dangerous road crossings.

Refreshments: Lots of choice in the centre of Peterborough; Boat House Inn, near to the rowing lake. Café at the Ferry Meadows Country Park.

Cycle Hire: At Lakeside Leisure, Ferry Meadows, to the west of Peterborough (at the western end of the route described), tel: 01733 234418.

ROUTE INSTRUCTIONS:
1. From the footbridge over the River Nene just south of the centre of Peterborough (by Asda and close to Railway World) turn right on Henry Penn Walk alongside the river (keeping the water to your left).

2. At the T-junction at the end of the tarmac turn right to cross the bridge then left by the Boat House Inn. Follow the path around the edge of the rowing lake, keeping the water to your left.

3. At the T-junction by the main road at the end of the lake turn left signposted 'Orton, Ferry Meadows'. Pass beneath the road bridge, over the river bridge, cross the railway line then turn right signposted 'Orton Meadows, Ferry Meadows, Lynch Wood'.

4. At the next T-junction turn right to cross the railway line then turn left. Cross the road with care then turn right on the tarmac path alongside the road to the Visitor Centre.

5. For a full circuit of the lakes follow signs for 'Bluebell Wood, Adventure Playground, Nature Reserve'.

6. To return to Peterborough along the south side of the River Nene, follow the tarmac path alongside the exit road from the park then turn left signposted 'Station, Orton Mere, City Centre'.

7. Keep following the tarmac path as it crosses the railway line then turn left parallel with the line, signposted 'Orton Mere, City Centre'.

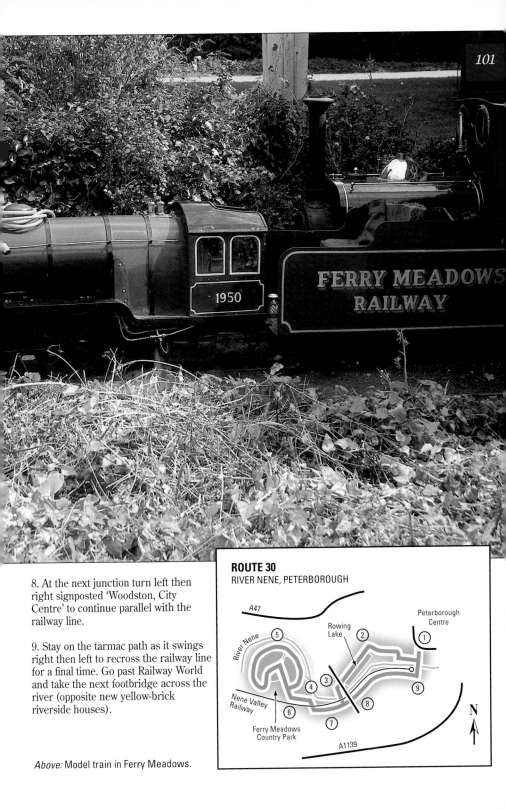

8. At the next junction turn left then right signposted 'Woodston, City Centre' to continue parallel with the railway line.

9. Stay on the tarmac path as it swings right then left to recross the railway line for a final time. Go past Railway World and take the next footbridge across the river (opposite new yellow-brick riverside houses).

ROUTE 30
RIVER NENE, PETERBOROUGH

A47

River Nene

Rowing Lake

Peterborough Centre

Nene Valley Railway

Ferry Meadows Country Park

A1139

N

Above: Model train in Ferry Meadows.

A. ROUTES IN THE FIRST *CYCLING WITHOUT TRAFFIC: THE MIDLANDS & PEAK DISTRICT*

The 29 routes below are described more fully in the first *Cycling Without Traffic: The Midlands & Peak District,* also published by Dial House, available from all good bookshops.

1. The Longdendale Trail, northeast of Glossop.
2. The Middlewood Way, north of Macclesfield.
3. The Sett Valley Trail, New Mills, south of Glossop.
4. The Upper Derwent Valley, between Sheffield and Manchester.
5. Tatton Park, north of Knutsford.
6. The Salt Line, Alsager, northwest of Stoke.
7. The Biddulph Valley Trail, south of Congleton to Biddulph.
8. Rudyard Lake, northwest of Leek.
9. The Monsal Trail, north of Bakewell.
10. The High Peak Trail, west of Matlock.
11. The Tissington Trail, north of Ashbourne.
12. The Manifold Trail, northwest of Ashbourne.
13. The Churnet Valley Trail, Oakamoor, west of Ashbourne.
14. Clumber Country Park, southeast of Worksop.
15. The Five Pits Trail, Temple Normanton, southeast of Chesterfield.
16. The Pleasley Trails, northwest of Mansfield.
17. Clipstone Forest, Sherwood, northeast of Mansfield.
18. Shipley Country Park, west of Nottingham.
19. Elvaston Castle Country Park, east of Derby.
20. The Stafford-Newport Greenway, west of Stafford.
21. North from Leicester to Watermead Park.
22. South from Leicester to Blaby.
23. A circuit of Rutland Water, east of Leicester.
24. The Brampton Valley Way, between Market Harborough and Northampton.
25. The Kingswinford Trail, Wombourne, southwest of Wolverhampton.
26. The Worcester & Birmingham Canal, southwest of Birmingham.
27. North from Worcester along the canal.
28. The River Severn through Worcester.
29. The Stratford Greenway, south of Stratford-upon-Avon.

Above: Many railway paths were described in the first volume of *Cycling Without Traffic: The Midlands & Peak District.*

Right: Bike hire at Clumber Park.

B. OTHER ROUTES IN BRIEF

Below is a further list of traffic-free routes in the region that I simply did not have the space to include in the main section. The brief description given for each of these routes should enable you to find the start of the trail and know what sort of ride you are likely to enjoy.

1. Clumber to Blidworth
A 17-mile section of Sustrans' National Route 6 from the edge of the Clumber Estate (just south of Worksop) through Clumber Park and across Sherwood Forest Country Park and Clipstone Forest to the edge of Blidworth (southeast of Mansfield).

2. Worksop Canal
A 3-mile section of canal towpath to the west of Worksop, as far as Shireoaks, also used on National Route 6.

3. Five Weirs Walk, Sheffield
A 6-mile circular ride along the banks of the River Don and the towpath of the Sheffield & South Yorkshire Canal from the heart of Sheffield northeast towards the M1 Jct 34. Please note that this trail is also very popular with walkers.

4. Washingborough to Skellingthorpe
Dismantled railways have been converted to create this traffic-free route from one side of Lincoln to the other.

C. LONG-DISTANCE TRAILS

1. The Trans-Pennine Trail
The 205-mile trail from Liverpool to Hull (Southport to Hornsea) is a high-quality trail for walkers, cyclists and, where possible, horse riders and disabled people. Linking the cities of Liverpool, Manchester, Sheffield, Leeds, York and Hull, it has been developed by 26 local authorities. It is also Route 62 of the National Cycle Network. In 1995 the Millennium Commission awarded a £5.3 million grant to enable the trail to be completed by the end of 2000. Many of the traffic-free sections are used in this book or are covered by the first *Cycling Without Traffic: The Midlands & Peak District* or *Cycling Without Traffic: The North*.

For further information contact the Trans-Pennine Trail Office, c/o Department of Planning, Barnsley Metropolitan Borough Council, Central Office, Kendray Street, Barnsley S70 2TN. Tel: 01226 772574.

2. The Viking Way
A long-distance trail from the Humber to Rutland Water using minor roads, tracks and paths. Many sections are bridleways or byways where you have a right to cycle. The quality varies but it is worth exploring the bridleways and byways on mountain bikes in summer, using the appropriate Ordnance Survey maps. Lincolnshire County Council produces a 'Viking Way' booklet costing £2.

D. CANAL TOWPATHS AND REGIONAL WATERWAYS BOARDS

The theory is that there are 2,000 miles of towpaths in England and Wales, offering flat, vehicle-free cycling. The reality is that only a fraction of the towpath network is suitable for cycling; the rest is too narrow, overgrown, muddy and rough. There is obviously much room for improvement and certain waterways boards, in conjunction with local authorities and the Countryside Commission, have made immense progress in improving towpaths for all user groups. However, even the areas which have a reasonable surface are often busy with anglers and walkers, so when cycling on canal towpaths, extra care and consideration are needed.

Within the book there are five rides on short sections of canal towpaths. For the rest of the canal network please refer to the map and to the addresses and phone numbers of the local waterways board covering your area. There is no overall guideline about cycling on towpaths: some authorities issue a permit and charge for it, others issue a free permit; some have opened up the whole towpath to cyclists, others allow cycling only on certain sections. The most up-to-date information can be obtained from your local waterways board.

The addresses and phone numbers are as follows:

■ **Cheshire**
British Waterways, Navigation Road, Northwich, Cheshire CW8 1BH.
Tel: 01606 723800.

■ **Leicestershire**
(see Nottinghamshire)

■ **Northamptonshire**
Grand Union Canal, Canal Central, The Stop House, The Wharf, Braunston, Northamptonshire NN11 7JQ.
Tel: 01788 704481.

■ **Nottinghamshire**
1. East Midlands Navigations, The Kiln, Mather Lane, Newark, Nottinghamshire NG24 1FB.
Tel: 01636 704481

2. Grand Union Canal North, Trent Lock, Lock Lane, Long Eaton, Nottingham NG10 2FF.
Tel: 0115 946 1017.

■ **Shropshire**
Border Counties Waterways, Canal Office, Birch Road, Ellesmere, Shropshire SY12 9AA.
Tel: 01691 622549.

Right: Barge along the Grand Union Canal.

Below: Would you rather share the route with sheep or cars?

Canal network of Midlands & Peak District

[Map showing canal network with locations: MANCHESTER, Manchester Ship, Macclesfield, Sheffield & S.Yorks, SHEFFIELD, Chesterfield, CHESTER, Shropshire, Union, Trent and Mersey, Caldon, STOKE-ON-TRENT, Erewash, Trent and Mersey, NOTTINGHAM, Birmingham Canal Navigations, Ashby, Coventry, BIRMINGHAM, LEICESTER, Staffs and Worcs, Stratford & Birmingham, Oxford, Grand Union, Worcester & Birmingham, Grand Union, Stratford, WORCESTER, STRATFORD UPON AVON, Oxford, NORTHAMPTON]

■ Staffordshire and Warwickshire
1. Trent & Mersey Canal,
Fradley Junction, Alrewas,
Burton upon Trent,
Staffordshire DE13 7DN.
Tel: 01283 790236.

2. Staffordshire & Shropshire
Union Canal,
Norbury Junction, Stafford ST20 0PN.
Tel: 01785 284253.

■ West Midlands
Birmingham & Black Country Canals,
Bayleys Lane, Tipton,
West Midlands DY4 0PX.
Tel: 0121 506 1300.

■ Worcestershire
Worcester & Birmingham Canal,
Brome Hall Lane, Lapworth, Solihull,
West Midlands B94 5RB.
Tel: 01564 784634.

THE WATERWAYS CODE
FOR CYCLISTS

1. Access paths can be steep and slippery — join the towing path with care.

2. Always give way to other people on the towing path and warn them of your approach, a 'hello' and 'thank you' mean a lot. Be prepared to dismount if the path is busy with pedestrians or anglers.

3. You must dismount and push your cycle if the path narrows, or passes beneath a low bridge or alongside a lock.

4. Ride at a gentle pace, in single file, and do not bunch.

5. Never race — you have water on one side of you.

6. Watch out when passing moored boats — there may be mooring spikes concealed on the path.

7. Take particular care on wet or uneven surfaces, and don't worsen them by skidding.

8. Never cycle along towing paths in the dark.

9. Towing paths are not generally suitable for organised cycling events, but the local Waterways Manager may give permission.

10. If you encounter a dangerous hazard, please notify the Waterways Manager at the regional office.

Please remember you are responsible for your own and others' safety! You are only allowed to cycle on towing paths if you follow this code.

FORESTRY
COMMISSION LAND

The Forestry Commission owns many thousands of acres of land in the area covered by this book and has, by and large, adopted an enlightened approach to cycling in its woodlands. The broad rule of thumb is that you are allowed to ride on the hard, stone-based forestry roads which provide excellent opportunities for safe, family cycling. You are NOT allowed to cycle in the woodland away from these hard tracks and should pay attention to any signs which may indicate a temporary or permanent restriction on cycling (normally on walkers' trails or where forestry operations are in progress).

Below: Traffic-free trails are a great place to learn to ride.

In some places, the forestry authorities have even waymarked a trail for cyclists. However, open access is not universally the case, and in some woodlands you are only allowed on tracks where there is a statutory right of way, namely bridleways and byways.

This may all sound a little confusing, but the Forestry Commission is extremely helpful and normally has good reasons for restricting access. The forests are working environments where heavy machinery is often being used to fell or plant trees and whenever work is in progress there will be restrictions on recreational use.

A phone call or a letter to your local Forest Enterprise office should clarify the situation (addresses and phone numbers are listed below). In order to simplify matters as much as possible, forestry areas have been divided into two categories:

(A) sites where a trail has been waymarked for cyclists;
(B) other sites.

The best maps to use for exploring Forestry Commission woodland are the most up-to-date Ordnance Survey 1:25,000 maps (Pathfinder/green, Explorer/orange, Outdoor Leisure/yellow).

PLEASE NOTE: It must be stressed that there are many different user groups enjoying the woodlands, so courtesy and consideration should be shown at all times to walkers and horse riders. The fact that a bike can travel faster than a pedestrian does not give you any priority; indeed, priority normally lies with the walker or the horse rider. Use a bell to give warning of your presence and say thank you to people who step aside for you.

(A) FORESTRY WITH WAYMARKED CYCLE TRAILS

There are seven waymarked trails on Forestry Commission land in the area covered by the book:
1. Wharncliffe Wood, near Sheffield (Route 12, page 48).
2. Clipstone Forest in Sherwood Forest Country Park, north of Nottingham (covered in the first *Cycling Without Traffic: The Midlands & Peak District*).
3. Delamere Forest, east of Chester (Route 7, page 34).

4. Cannock Chase, north of Birmingham (Route 23, page 78).
5. Colstey Woods/Bury Ditches, Shropshire (25 miles south of Shrewsbury, Grid Reference 334838).
6. Eastridge Woods/Habberley/Poles Coppice car park (10 miles southwest of Shrewsbury, Grid Reference 386043).
7. Hopton Woods near Craven Arms, Shropshire (10 miles west of Ludlow, Grid Reference 350779).

(B) OTHER FORESTRY AREAS

In addition to the waymarked forestry trails listed above there are many small Forest Enterprise holdings throughout the Midlands where it would be possible to devise your own routes on the forestry roads. These are concentrated:

1. To the east of Mansfield (around Sherwood Forest).
2. North and east of Peterborough.
3. To the west of Ludlow in Shropshire.

The best publication showing all these holdings is a 48-page A4 booklet called *Ramblers' Atlas of Public Forests* published by the Ramblers' Association. It is available free by sending a large (A4) stamped addressed envelope with 52p of stamps to: Ramblers' Association, 1/5 Wandsworth Road, London SW8 2XX. This together with the appropriate Ordnance Survey Landranger (1:50,000) or Explorer (1:25,000) map will allow you to see your options and plan your routes.

Above: Route planning for beginners.

It is also worth contacting the following Forest Enterprise District Offices for further information:

- Sherwood & Lincolnshire Forest District, Edwinstowe, Mansfield, Nottinghamshire NG21 9JL. Tel: 01842 810271

- Northants Forest District, Top Lodge, Fineshade, Corby, Northamptonshire NN17 3BB. Tel: 01780 444394

- West Midlands Forest District, Lady Hill, Birches Valley, Rugeley, Staffordshire WS15 2UQ. Tel: 01889 586593

SUSTRANS' NATIONAL CYCLE NETWORK

The National Cycle Network is a linked series of traffic-free paths and traffic-calmed roads being developed right across the United Kingdom, linking town centres and the countryside. 5000 miles (the Millennium Routes) are open in 2000 and a further 5000 miles will open by 2005.

Below: One way of carrying your picnic.

In the region covered by this book there are three long sections of the National Cycle Network that are open in 2000:

1. **The Trans-Pennine Trail** — see Long-Distance Trails above.

2. **Barnsley to Derby and Milton Keynes.** National Route 6 links several traffic-free sections on its way south across the Midlands. Within the main section of this book you will find Rother Valley Country Park, the Chesterfield Canal, Clumber Park, Derby to Worthington and the Grand Union Canal near Market Harborough. Other sections such as the Brampton Valley Way were covered by the previous *Cycling Without Traffic: The Midlands & Peak District.*

3. **Derby-Birmingham-Banbury-Oxford.** The National Cycle Network branches into two as it heads south from Derby, rejoining in Kidlington, north of Oxford. This western route runs southwest through Burton upon Trent and Lichfield to Birmingham where it joins the traffic-free Birmingham Canal Towpath (Route 25) and the Rea Valley Route (Route 27). South of Birmingham the route uses a short traffic-free section down the Arrow Valley in Redditch then a longer dismantled railway section south of Stratford-upon-Avon (the Stratford Greenway).

LOCAL AUTHORITY LEAFLETS

Local authorities often produce cycling leaflets, such as town maps showing urban cycle networks or leaflets describing recreational routes in the countryside. However, when trying to obtain these leaflets, do not expect any logic or consistency: not only does the quantity and quality of leaflets vary from one authority to the next but each authority seems to have a different name for the department in charge of cycling! In addition, some charge for their leaflets and some give them away free. Just to complicate matters further, local authorities are forever reorganising and changing department names, then of course leaflets run out and are not reprinted...

As you can see it would be very easy to give information that would be out of date almost as soon as the book is published, so instead it is suggested that you become the detective and find out from your own local authority what cycling leaflets they have produced. Below is a list of the addresses and main telephone numbers of each of the local authorities (County Councils, Metropolitan Councils, Unitary Authorities) in the area covered by this book.

When you call, ask to speak to 'The Cycling Officer' or to someone about recreational or family cycling. You may be put through to one of the following departments: Planning, Highways, Tourism, Transport, Environment, Access & Recreation, or Countryside Section and do not be surprised to be transferred from one department to another! Have a pen and paper handy so that when you do get through to the right person you can note down their name and their direct phone line and the address to which you should send money (if required). They may also be able to help you with the names of people to speak to in the adjoining authorities.

An alternative to this is to contact Sustrans Information Service, PO Box 21, Bristol BS99 2HA (Tel: 0117 929 0888) or visit its website at www.sustrans.org.uk. For a small handling fee they should be able to provide you with the leaflets you require.

LOCAL AUTHORITIES' ADDRESSES AND TELEPHONE NUMBERS

Barnsley
Town Hall, Barnsley S70 2TA.
Tel: 01226 770770.

Birmingham City
Council House, Victoria Square,
Birmingham B1 1BB. Tel: 0121 303 2000.

Cheshire
County Hall, Chester CH1 1SF.
Tel: 01244 602424.

Coventry
Council House, Earl Street,
Coventry CV1 5RS. Tel: 024 7683 3333.

Derby City
Council House, Corporation Street,
Derby DE1 2FS. Tel: 01332 293111.

Derbyshire
County Hall, Matlock, Derbyshire DE4 3AG.
Tel: 01629 580000.

Doncaster
Council House, Doncaster DN1 3JE.
Tel: 01302 734305.

Dudley
Council House, Priory Road, Dudley DY1
1HF. Tel: 01384 818181.

Herefordshire
Brocklington, 35 Hafod Road,
Hereford HR1 1SH. Tel: 01432 260000.

Leicester City
Welford Place, Leicester LE1 6ZG.
Tel: 0116 254 9922.

Leicestershire
County Hall, Glenfield, Leicester LE3 8RA.
Tel: 0116 232 3232.

Lincolnshire
Newland, Lincoln LN1 1YL.
Tel: 01522 552222.

Liverpool
Municipal Buildings, Dale Street, Liverpool
L69 2DH. Tel: 0151 227 3911.

Manchester
City Council, Town Hall,
Manchester M60 2LA. Tel: 0161 234 5000.

Northamptonshire
County Hall, Northampton NN1 1DN.
Tel: 01604 236236.

North Lincolnshire
Pittwood House, Ashby Road,
Scunthorpe DN16 1AB. Tel: 01724 296296.

Nottingham City
Guildhall, Nottingham NG1 4BT.
Tel: 0115 915 5555.

Nottinghamshire
County Hall, West Bridgford, Nottingham
NG2 7QP. Tel: 0115 982 3823.

Peterborough
Town Hall, Bridge Street,
Peterborough PE1 1HG. Tel: 01733 563141.

Rotherham
Civic Building, Walker Place,
Rotherham S65 1UF. Tel: 01709 382121.

Rutland
Council Offices, Catmose, Oakham LE1 6HP.
Tel: 01572 722577.

Sandwell
Wigmore Buildings, Penny Hill Lane,
West Bromwich B71 3RZ. Tel: 0121 569 4095.

Sheffield
Town Hall, Sheffield S1 2HH.
Tel: 0114 273 4552.

Shropshire
Shire Hall, Abbey Foregate,
Shrewsbury SY2 6ND. Tel: 01743 251000.

Solihull
Council House, Solihull,
West Midlands B91 3QS. Tel: 0121 704 6000.

Staffordshire
County Buildings, Martin Street, Stafford
ST16 2LH. Tel: 01785 223121

Stockport
Town Hall, Stockport SK1 3XE.
Tel: 0161 342 8355 [check].

Stoke-on-Trent
Civic Centre, Glebe Street,
Stoke-on-Trent ST4 1RN. Tel: 01782 234567.

Tameside
Wellington Road,
Ashton-under-Lyne OL6 6DL.
Tel: 0161 342 8355.

Telford & Wrekin
Civic Offices, Telford TF3 4LD.
Tel: 01952 202100.

Trafford
Town Hall, Talbot Road, Trafford M32 0YT.
Tel: 0161 912 1212.

Walsall
Civic Centre, Darwall Street,
Walsall WS1 1TP. Tel: 01922 650000.

Warrington
Town Hall, Warrington WA1 1UH.
Tel: 01925 444400.

Warwickshire
Shire Hall, Warwick CV34 4TH.
Tel: 01926 412022.

Wirral
Town Hall, Brighton Street,
Wallasey L44 8ED. Tel: 0151 638 7070.

Wolverhampton
Civic Centre, St Peters Square,
Wolverhampton WV1 1SH. Tel: 01902 556556.

Worcestershire
County Hall, Spetchley Road,
Worcester WR2 2NP. Tel: 01905 763763.

TOURIST INFORMATION CENTRES

Another option in your quest for further cycling information is to contact the Tourist Information Centres covering the area in which you are interested. They frequently stock local leaflets and booklets that don't find their way into bookshops or any form of national distribution. Their numbers are listed below.

Barnsley	01226 206757
Birmingham	0121 643 2514
Buxton	01298 25106
Cambridge	01223 322640
Chester	01244 322220
Coventry	024 7683 2303
Derby	01332 255802
Leicester	0116 265 0555
Lincoln	01522 529828
Liverpool	0151 708 8854
Manchester	0161 234 3157
Northampton	01604 622677
Nottingham	0115 915 5330
Peterborough	01733 452336
Sheffield	0114 273 4671
Shrewsbury	01743 350761
Stoke-on-Trent	01782 284600
Worcester	01905 726311

OTHER USEFUL ADDRESSES

Cyclists Touring Club (CTC)
Britain's largest cycling organisation, promoting recreational and utility cycling. The CTC provides touring and technical advice, legal aid and insurance and campaigns to improve facilities and opportunities for all cyclists. CTC, Cotterrell House, 69 Meadrow, Godalming, Surrey GU7 3HS. Tel: 01483 417217.

Cycle Campaign Network
National liaison organisation, bringing together information about Britain's many local cycle campaigns. For details of your local campaign group send an SAE to: CCN, 54-57 Allison Street, Digbeth, Birmingham B5 5TH.

Sustrans Information Service
PO Box 21, Bristol BS99 2HA. Tel: 0117 929 0888. In 1995 Sustrans won £43 million of lottery funds to help build the 10,000-mile National Cycle Network which will be completed by the year 2005. The Millennium Routes, covering the first 5000 miles of the Network open in 2000, include a route stretching from Dover to Inverness. The network uses a mixture of quiet lanes, forestry tracks, canal towpaths, dismantled railways and purpose-built cycleways.

Above: Escape into the countryside.